THE LONG WAIT

THE STORY OF WILLIAM WYATT PATTON JR.
3rd Scouting Force - 8th USAAF

E. Richard Atkins
LT. COL. USAF (RET)

authorHOUSE®

AuthorHouse™
1663 Liberty Drive
Bloomington, IN 47403
www.authorhouse.com
Phone: 1 (800) 839-8640

Published by AuthorHouse 12/26/2017

ISBN: 978-1-5462-0042-0 (sc)
ISBN: 978-1-5462-0041-3 (e)

Library of Congress Control Number: 2017911664

CONTENTS

"DO NOT STAND AT MY GRAVE AND WEEP
I AM NOT THERE, I DO NOT SLEEP"

DEDICATION

This book is dedicated to the memory of William Wyatt Patton Jr.
And all who love him

FOREWORD

This is one of the saddest stories of World War II. It is the tale of a man who loved the military; a man who excelled at every turn; one who gave every ounce of energy to serve his country only to be dogged by a litany of misfortune.

True, war brings some element of misfortune to many who are selected to serve. The death of a soldier always brings pain and anguish to the family but, there is ultimately healing for It is said, "Time heals all wounds." But closure is denied by that terrible classification: "Missing In Action." It is the beginning of severe and lasting pain for those who loved.

This is an extreme case and but one which should have never taken place. Young William Wyatt Patton Jr. gave his life in the last full measure of devotion only to be failed in death by the country he loved so dearly.

He died in a lonely marsh in northern France and rested there for 56 years, waiting for those he served to care. Ultimately, serendipity was to write the closing chapter with a French Farmers shovel.

A case of gross incompetence. Strong words you say…judge for yourself: He was reported down by his flight leader and the location pin pointed. The wreckage was examined by French and American Military the following day… yet no one searched for the pilot. Of those official US Army files that were found and provided to the family there is no evidence that Graves Registration was ever notified nor that a search was ever conducted by any military organization.

To the contrary, the file is filled with Army forms and minutes of Review Board meetings, concluding that there was really no point in searching for him. From the minutes of the 7887th Graves Registration Detachment dated 7 December 1950 I quote: ***"Due to the absence of visual evidence relative to the aircraft having crashed in the area cited, no specific field investigation could be initiated."***

In a final irony, Patton's official Deceased Identification File was recently lost by the Army and has not been located at the time of this writing.

PREFACE

This volume, like **FIGHTING SCOUTS OF THE 8ᵀᴴ AIR FORCE,**
the Scouting Force history, began as an effort to record the history of an
unusual event, the finding of a World War II Airman who was Missing
in Action for 56 years. Instead, "lightning struck" for a second time

Like my association with the 8ᵗʰ Air Force Scouts of World War II,
writing the Patton story turned into a personal and meaningful event.
Just as the Scouts became an extension of my family, so too, the Pattons
have become just as dear to wife Marian and I!

In France, another extended family has been formed. The wonderful
people of La Longueville, Feignies, Maubeuge and the surrounding area
have reached across the Atlantic, in spirit, to find a place in our hearts.
Their adoration of William Patton has been made manifest in their
memorials and the marvelous museum created in his honor.

Even more dramatic, has been my association with William Wyatt
Patton Jr., whom I now know as though we had been raised together.
Though we never met and he has been gone for 56 years, he is very
real to me. His story, a dichotomy of success and sadness, is now a
permanent part of my life.

It is obvious that GOD wanted your author to chronicle the patton saga as he provided contacts and created events that could not be explained in any other way. he has allowed this fallen hero to reach out from the grave and lead me in a fashion that could happen only through divine guidance

SPECIAL THANKS

This book has been made possible through the the inspiration, encouragement and material provided by Connie Patton. From the day we first met Connie and the Patton family in April 2001, to her most recent visit to the Atkins home in June 2007, she has been a full partner in making this chronicle come to light.

It all began at the first meeting with the family. Connie produced the box of documents and artifacts which became the foundation for "Junior" Patton's long overdue biography. The material was there and the inspiration soon followed. From that point on we were in constant contact and the flow of material continued. She provided an incredible base from which to begin the research.

CONNIE PATTON

Connie established communications with the French citizens of the crash site communities and attended 2003 & 2005 memorial ceremonies in the La Longueville, Feignies, Maubage area. She took many photographs and made them available along with her observations and many stories about her visits.

After seeing the magnificent William W. Patton Museum in France, she was dedicated to bringing portions of "Junior's" P-51 Mustang to

United States so that American citizens could benefit from its display. Over a 3 year period, working with Missouri Congressman Roy Blunt's staff and the Air and Military Museum of Springfield, Missouri, the complex issues of US and French Customs and the logistics of packing and transportation were solved and the display opened in November 2005.

The final Scouting Force reunion was held in conjunction with the 2006 reunion of the 8th Air Force Historical Society, near the current 8AF headquarters, in Bossier City, Louisiana. 6 Scouting Force veterans were in attendance (5 from the 3rd Scouts) and "Junior" was there in spirit. Connie brought her brother and his family plus 2 large boxes of documents and artifacts. Brand new finds for me to pour over!

In June 2007, Connie visited the Atkins family in Texas and the conversation was easy to predict. We poured over documents, pictures and artifacts. It was a great time for all and we were able to summarize the activities of the past 6 years and document via video.

Again, thanks to Connie's help, another tile is placed in the massive mosaic of history.

ACKNOWLEDGEMENT

Acknowledgements in published works are generally confined to a page or less, crammed together to save paper and give the impression that they rank rather low priority. This seldom the choice of the writer but considered by the publisher to be an economic necessity. Since it would have been impossible to prepare a comprehensive and authentic story without the help of many, I feel that the contributors to this volume deserve to be singled out and recognized as members of the story team. So here they are, give them a hearty cheer!

PATTON FAMILY

The Patton family is the heart of this story content but more importantly, has provided a friendship that makes the William W. Patton saga very personal to the Atkins family. We owe a great debt of gratitude to these wonderful folks for accepting us into their inner circle of sadness and joy that IS the story

It all began with the discovery of the Patton family in Neosho, Missouri and our first visit with the dynamic quartet which consists of William Patton's Sister-in-law, **Margaret Patton** and William's nieces **Connie Patton**, **Donna Patton Brown** and **Joyce Patton Montez**. These ladies supplied not only the personal stories and documentation, they provided the inspiration for this volume to be a labor of love as well as a historical piece.

We were later to meet niece **Joan Taylor Spee**, who visited the crash site immediately after the discovery And who provided a personal account of her visit to the crash site soon after the discovery.

Other Patton nephews & nieces include **Darrell** and **Gary Patton, Sharon Patton Cochran, Debbie Patton Vogt**, **Mike Taylor and** Brother-in-law, **Reverend Norman Taylor,**

Ross Langley is a cousin who knew William better than anyone, having lived with the family and having served with Patton in the Army Air Force for many years. Ross was able to give a close up and personal picture of Patton.

SCOUTING FORCE ASSOCIATION

Over the years, veterans of the 1st, 2nd and 3rd Scouting Force gathered under the banner of the Scouting Force Association to once again enjoy fellowship and relive the days of their wartime exploits. Annual reunions and individual gatherings were enjoyed by all.

Under the leadership Of **Colonel Ed Beaty**, former 447th Bomb Group B-17 combat pilot and Operations Officer of the 3rd Scouts, funds were donated by the Scouts to assure publication of the Patton story and Volume 2 of the Scouting Force history. To Ed and all of the Association members, your author is deeply indebted. They made it possible to document the operations of an organization that made a major contribution to the winning go of World War II and which went undocumented

MILITARY COMRADES

We were very fortunate in being able to locate many who served with William Patton during his distinguished military career during the 1934-1945 period in the United States, Hawaii and in England.

Hawaii Service-5th Bomb Group

This is a special group of comrades who shared the horrors and heroics of 7 December 1941 during the cowardly Japanese attack on Pearl Harbor. Included in this wonderful group of comrades is **Doug Allen, Byram Bates, Donald Bloomfield, Joe Peseck, Elman Lemley, Dick Modling, Wm. H. Stewart (for David Miller) and Charles Werntz.** These fine fellows provided great insight into Patton's personality as well as a vivid description of their actions during the Japanese attack.

Cadet Classmates

Another who played a major role in William Patton's life story, beginning with service in Hawaii and the Day Of Infamy, was **Doug Hicks**. Doug was a comrade-in-arms and friend for almost 10 years, having met him in Hawaii, going thru Pilot Training together and serving in the 94th Bomb group in England. As fate would have it, Jim lived just 3 blocks from the Author's house! What a great time we had remembering Patton. **Jim Shawhan**, a Patton classmate all thru pilot training, was located thru a letter mailed to the Patton family in 1944. A search of the Internet located Jim in Southwest Indiana. It so happened that my wife and I were going to our annual family reunion in Southwest Indiana and the Shawhans lived just 20 miles from the reunion site! What a great time we had with the Shawhans. **Charles O'Mahoney, Maurice Neher,** and **Floren Nelson** are 3 more Patton classmates that I located via the Internet. They all went to B-26 Marauders, flying many combat missions and having A very exciting war. **Charles** is an accomplished author and chronicled their adventures in a book titled **BLUE BATTLEFIELDS**, published IN 1994 by AVIATION USK in Usk, Washington. It can be found under ISBN3080 0-9623080-6-4. His stories and photographs can also be found in many aviation periodicals

94th Bomb Group Personnel

Pilots **Doug Hicks** and **Bob Allison** both flew on a number of the June 1944 missions in the same formation with William Patton. Their combat experiences exemplified the dangers of the bomber war.

94th Bomb Group Association

Debi Robinson, President, and **all of the members** of the 94th Association were always available to assist in my research

388th Bomb Group Association

Jan Pack, 388th Site Webmaster and Association Presidents Richard Timberlake and Bob Ward and **all of the members** of the 388th Association were always ready to lend a hand.

Aphrodite Project-388th Bomb Group personnel

My earliest contact was **John Lansing**, project pioneer and control aircraft pilot, was able to give me a good overview of the Aphrodite project. Later I found **Fain Pool**, the very first pilot to fly an Aphrodite Jump Mission and further expanded my knowledge base. **John Hinner** was Patton's Co-pilot on mission 12 but had no recollection of the event. **Ken Waters,** who flew the jump aircraft on mission 16, was kind enough to allow me to quote from his personal diary. Finally, I made contact with **Charles Beck** who was a ground crewman on B-17 named "Gremlin Gus." This was known as the "roadster" because the top of the cockpit had been removed.

55th Fighter Group

Lt. Herman Schoenberg was assigned to the 55th Fighter Group "Clobber College" at their Wormingford base and was the instructor who checked-out Lt. Patton in the P-51 Mustang. He was very helpful in picturing the role of the organization and his duties there. **Millard Anderson**, 55 FG Ops Officer, certified Lt. Patton as a qualified Mustang pilot. While Anderson had passed on some years back, Mrs.

Anderson was kind enough to provide information on her husband's career and a nice photograph.

3rd Scouting Force

My very first inquiries regarding Patton's Scouting Force service were directed at veteran 3rd Scouts **Ed Beaty, Noel Garvin, OV Lancaster and Cliff Manlove.** While none recalled serving with Patton, they were very helpful in developing the story background and evaluating my view of the events

US Air Force History Office, Washington, DC

Dr.Richard Hallion, Historian of the Air Force, an old friend, provided the assistance of his office plus his usual sage observations. The US Government is indeed fortunate to have such a brilliant man in their fold. **Col. George Ballinger**, of the USAF History Office at Bolling AFB, DC., was the first to alert me of the Patton affair via inquiries regarding his status with the Scouting Force. **Maj. John Beaulieu,** also of the USAF History Office was very helpful in guiding me to vital sources of information within the government.

US Air Force Historical Research Agency, Maxwell AFB, Alabama

One of the prime sources of data also provided great assistance though. **Mrs. Lynn Oliver Gamma,** Archivist of the Air Force. Always, friend of the historian she was very helpful as was **SMSGT Gary McDaniel**, Research Specialist, who handled so many individual requests with courtesy and dispatch. Both went "the extra mile" to expedite much needed data.

US Total Army Personnel Command, Alexandria Virginia

Liz Tate was instrumental in providing Individual Deceased Personnel Files which were so important to the story.

KEY CONTRIBUTORS

The Chief of Staff

Wife Marian Atkins, once again, stepped forward to man the dreaded computer, listen to a million war stories and provide the type of inspiration and comfort that only a wife can understand. Though my love for flying has been replaced by the recording of historical aviation events, she is still mystified by the "labor-of-love" justification. I suspect that she is not terribly unique amongst the wifely community. But she hangs in there....for 75 years to date!

MARIAN ATKINS

Stallion 51 Corporation

Solving the riddle of the crash dynamics of Patton's Mustang was a knotty issue which was brought into focus **by Lee Lauderback of the Stallion 51 Company**. Lee is a true expert on the P-51 and especially the spin characteristics.

Friends in France

Adjutant **Michel Archimbault,** head of the Gendermerie of Feignies, France, was the key French official in the Patton crash investigation and provided valuable assistance to the author. Journalist **Martine Kaczmarek** of Lilles **LA VOIX DU NORD** newspaper, provided news articles, photographs and valuable information. **Guillaume Lamaitte**, a young pilot and historian, also provided photographs and much other material and was a key figure in the development of the Patton Museum at Fort. There are many others, in fact most of the population of the La Longueville, Feignies, Maubage area, the historical organizations, the historians, the government agencies, the military and the citizenry of France are William W. Patton Jr. friends. *How wonderful it is to see* *an illustration of pure humanity transcend all of the other elements of this troubled planet!*

English Friends

Anthony Plowright, who located the elusive 94BG/331BS Crew load Lists for March thru July 1944 and made it available to me as a key research tool.

Peter Randall, historian, friend and creator of the "Little Friends" website http://www.littlefriends.co.uk which includes the history of the Scouting Force. Peter has represented myself and the Scouts at memorials honoring William Patton in 2001 and 2003. Peter was also there during the excavation of the crash site. He furnished many photographs used in this document. **Karina Herve,** Peters's daughter, who lives in Maubeuge, France, just a few miles from the crash site, slogged through the mud and endured the constant rain to take photos and give us reports on the progress of the excavation.

WILLIAM WYATT PATTON, JR

That smile tells the story
of
the beautiful personality and exceptional
charisma of this young warrior.
Though his life was short he is an icon of the Greatest Generation

INTRODUCTION

In this story you will meet a handsome young man of great character, incredible devotion to duty and a personality that endeared him to all who ever met him. He had a smile that lighted up the countryside

William Wyatt Patton Jr. was indeed a "cut above" the average fellow and left a trail of friends and acquaintances who remember him as "one of the nicest people I have ever known." Not only that, every piece of paper I uncovered and everyone who knew him personally, described him as "an outstanding soldier." Commendations and rapid promotion, unheard of in the pre-World War II army, were commonplace in Patton's career.

His story begins with a telephone call from the US Air Force History Office in Washington, DC, stating that Lt. Patton's remains had been found in France and their office was seeking information about his assignment as a member of the 3rd Scouting Force of the 8th Air Force, an organization for which I am the historian. I did not have Patton on my list of Scouts, in fact, had never heard the name. I immediately began a series of phone conversations with 3SF veterans to determine if any of the fellows remembered Patton and the fatal mission. Thus began the initial mystery for not a single one of the Scouts remembered him or the accident. Acquisition of the MACR (Missing Air Crew Report) confirmed that Patton was, indeed, a member of the 3rd Scouting Force. So the search for data began.

I was fortunate to locate quickly the Patton family in Missouri and to begin and enduring friendship while chronicling the sad saga of William Wyatt Patton Junior. Our first meeting in the home of Patton Sister-in-law Margaret Patton, included Margaret plus Nieces Donna, Joyce and Connie. It was a wonderful occasion, punctuated with memories both happy and sad. Fortunately the family was able to provide many documents and photographs of William Patton Jr. and the Patton family. It was at this gathering that it was revealed that the family's pet name for William was "Junior."

After pouring over the wealth of data provided by the family, the thought of a biography came to me and, with the encouragement of the family, the project was launched….not so much a literary effort as it is a labor of love in memory of a gallant warrior.

Writing is work but the real pleasure for a historian is the research. It is especially pleasing when so much of the effort is associated with the people who are directly involved in the creation of the story.

Attending the memorial services, meeting other family members, locating Patton's comrades, uncovering his military history and establishing a link with his French "family" were elements that made this a very rewarding venture. So, after 5 years of research and writing, the goal is finally reached.

> **But the greatest reward was getting to know Junior Patton Today it is as if I had known him all of my life.**

PART I

DISCOVERY

CRASH SITE

CHAPTER 1

DISCOVERY

On 18 February 2001, A French Farmer, draining a swampy field in order to eventually return it to service, unearths the wreckage of an airplane. To the shock and surprise of all involved, it turns out to be an American fighter aircraft that still holds the remains of the pilot. Little did he realize that he had found the answer to a mystery of 56 years.

FINDING LT. PATTON

For years, a little patch of soil in Fiegnies, France lay dormant as it was filled with water and, for most of that period, recovery was not economical. On 18 February 2001, Messr. Luc Druet, Farmer of the field designated as plot 2295, decided that the time had come to return this field to agricultural usage. He pulled on his heavy coat to protect against the chill winds of February, mounted his backhoe equipped tractor and set about the task of cutting ditches through the flooded ground.

The tractor splashes its way across the water soaked land, threatening to sink at any moment in the spongy soil. Suddenly, there is a wrenching sound as metal encounters metal. Much to Druet's suprise, a rusted machine gun appeared. He ceased the plowing. Returning home after working his field he discussed it with an acquaintance, which shall hereafter be referred to as Messr X for legal reasons.

The following morning, in a totally unauthorized move, the acquaintance, Messr X, returned with a Backhoe and for the next 4 days, proceeded to cut trenches across the field, unearthing a great many aircraft parts and human remains. *Thus, he forever eliminated any possibility of a controlled archeological dig. Messr X destroyed some of the aircraft through this thoughtless process and denied history a valuable artifact and evidence critical to the crash investigation. Like many who do not understand the art and science of investigation, his intention was probably limited to the gathering a few war souvenirs and did not realize the damage he had inflicted on this hallowed site.*

Upon discovery, Messr Druet, shocked by the thoughtless action of his neighbor, contacted the local Gendarmerie in Feignies. The Gendarmerie officer-in-charge, Adjutant Michel Archimbault, immediately launched an investigation. Messr X was contacted and initially denied his actions. Subsequently, it was reported to Adjutant Archimbault that Messr. X had a parachute in his possession. Archimbault immediately returned to Messr. X and convinced him that criminal action might result if the truth was not forthcoming. Messr X then revealed the possession of a military Identification tag bearing the name of Patton, a bag of what appeared to be human remains and pilot personal effects.

The American authorities were notified and assembly of the official team began. The investigation was conducted by the United States Army Central Investigation Laboratory located at Hick ham Air Force Base in Hawaii, assisted by Air Force personnel from German bases and the American Embassy in Paris.

LUC DRUET

THE MAN WHO DISCOVERED THE PATTON CRASH SITE

CRASH AREA

The setting for this drama is about 45 miles from the city of Lille and just 3 miles from the Belgian border. It is an area that knows the ravages of modern war all to well as it was in the midst of World Wars I and II. Here now was another graphic reminder of World War II. The site is closest to the town of La Longueville and near Feignies and Maubeuge.

I AM ALERTED OF THIS SITUATION BY MESSAGES FROM THE PENTAGON

I was personally drawn into this story as the result of a message from the US Air Force History office. This because of my position as historian of the Scouting Forces of the 8th Air Force. I had heard of the discovery and, as a historian, I was interested but I did not know how deeply I was to be involved when I read the following message:

27 February 2001-Initial message from Colonel Ballinger – *"Sir, last night there was a piece on the NBC nightly news about the recent discovery of a WWII aircraft and the remains of a US pilot. We believe the aircraft was a P-51D (SN: 44-15331) and the remains may be those of 1Lt William W. Patton, Jr. Of course, all of this is unconfirmed, but I was wondering if you would have any info that might help. Was Lt Patton in your unit, the 3rd Scouting Force? If so, do you remember when he was lost? Can you provide any additional info? We have a Missing Aircrew Report that Lt Patton was lost on 15 Jan 1945, near Roubaix, France."*

Having studied this organization for the past 20 years and being with most of the survivors many times and I consider Scouts an extension of my own family. As a result I know all of the names by heart and Patton was not a name I had ever heard in connection with the Scouting Force. *However, from this moment on, the name William Patton was to be burned into my memory and my heart forever.* I immediately responded with the following:

27 February 2001 -Response to Colonel Ballinger – *"I read about it in the newspaper and saw the NBC program. I received your message I went to the files to take a look at my documents to see if I could help. Found the following but do not think it will be of much value to you: From the serial number you provided I can identify it as a P-51D-15NA but it was not from the any of the 3 Scouting Forces nor was Lt. Patton. Roger Freeman's WAR DIARY shows a single loss each from the 78thFG and 55thFG (the 55th supported the 3rd Scouts) on 15 January 1945. However, the 55FG histories show NO losses on the 15th. Unfortunately, I do not have 78FG history. I have a suspicion that it was not a combat mission as he was dressed in class A's, complete with tie and wings. Bet he was on an R&R visit to France. What fighter group does the MACR show? Would you send me a copy as an e-mail message attachment? I will continue to poke around on this subject"*

29 February 2001- from Colonel Ballinger –*"Mr. Atkins: sir, thanks for getting back to me. The MACR is nearly illegible so I can't send it to you. But let me provide you with some of the more salient points. The MACR was dated 18 Jan 1945 and signed by Maj. Stanley E. Gagon, Ops Officer. The report was based on the eyewitness account of 1st Lt Bryan J. Booker. The organizational data states 8th AF, 3rd Air Division, 388th Bomb Group, 560th Bomb Squadron, with detached service to the 3rd Scouting Force. Place of departure was Wormingford. The incident occurred at 1115 on 15 Jan 1945. Weather conditions were strato cumulus at 1500' and ground fog at 1200'. The aircraft was believed to have been lost "while making 180 degree turn in fog, while separated from leader, believed to have spun-in."*

I also sent a message to my good friend and college, English Historian Extraordinaire Peter Randall, who operates our Scouting Force Website, Fighting Scouts of the Eighth Air Force at *http://homepages.tesco. net/~jrandall*. I informed him of the events taking place.

I received a message from Peter, which reads, in part: *"I received a phone call about this one as the wreck was found very near to where she is living. Facts so far: Wreck is of P-51. Remains of aircraft include parachute in the cockpit along with uniform/flying gear and, of course, human remains.*

Pilot identified by dog tags as Lt. William W. Patton posted as MIA on 15 January 1945. Records(on Wall of Missing at Madingly) give his unit as 388th BG 560th BS, a B-17 unit. Chances are he was a 3rd Scout as only unaccounted missing P-51 that day was from the 55th Fighter Group. My MACR book gives the loss but no pilot details or serial number of P-51. Current, research by guys on the Net, seem to indicate that MACR number 11919 is the relevant document but I have no record of this one. Looks possible that he could have been a transferee to the 3SF".

Knowing Peter has been a real pleasure as both friend and world class historian and in this instance, was a real stroke of good fortune. In addition, his daughter lived in France not 10 miles from the crash site, in the town of Maubeuge! Later she and Peter were able to visit the site, take photographs and interview the locals, in their own language, a very important aspect of getting a clear story. I did finally obtain a copy of Missing Air Crew Report(MACR) 11919 which left no doubt that Patton was indeed, a member of the 3rd Scouting Force. The challenge was now to obtain Patton's background, to try and determine what happened on that fateful day in January 1945 and to uncover the facts regarding the 56 year delay in finding him.

FRENCH FRIENDS

Determining the events surrounding the crash began at the crash site and involved several who were to become new friends. Though we have never met personally there is a bond which developed through this story. I would hope some day I might have the opportunity to return to France for a joyous gathering of this fine group. They include but are not limited to:

FeignIes Gendermarie Chief, Adjutant Michel Archimbault- Soon after, I received E-Mail from the central figure in the official aspects of the Patton story, Chief of the FeigInes Gendermarie, Adjutant Michel Archimbault. From this, began an exchange of messages related to the feelings of the community for this event. It was obvious that the local citizens were very emotionally involved. This is easy to understand as this area has been ravaged by war through many centuries

Journalist Martine Kaczmarek - Another very important figure in the Patton story, a Journalist for the **La Voix du Nord** newspaper. Martine was the principal French print journalist covering this incredible story. Thru E-Mail we became friends and her assistance in providing on-site data and research material was invaluable.

Historian and aviation enthusiast Guillaume LeMaitte - Guillaume was one of the local folks who assisted the authorities in excavation of the crash site and building of the Patton museum at Fort Leveau. Guillaume was a tremendous help in researching various aspects of the Patton story and supplying me with photographs and text. Guillaume and I have kept in constant contact since the very beginning of this story.

THE MEDIA AND OTHERS WEIGH IN

This story soon caught the fancy of the world media as. When aroused, they are like a pack of frenzied sharks at feeding time, attacking everyone and everything in sight. Finding Patton's airplane took place on 22 February and by the 23rd, the hunt was on!

The Allegedly Bullet Riddled Aircraft

In addition, the same Bulletin Board discussion picked up reports from an English Journalist who reported Patton's airplane and clothing as "bullet riddled." This made for a more dramatic story but made no sense when all of the facts at hand were ultimately reviewed. I believe that it was an honest mistake based on a hole in the engine and a hole in the Patton's neck scarf which were assumed to be bullet holes in the excitement and emotion of the moment. The events described in the MACR considered, attack by an enemy airplane is so remote a possibility as to not be considered a valid option. As you read further you will see that the accident was not comabat related.

MICHEL AND CATHY ARCHIMBAULT
As Commander of the Feignies Gendarmerie Adlutant Archimbault
was in charge of the crash site investigation. As with all who
participated, it was an emotional journey for Michel and Cathy

JOURNALIST MARTINE KACZMAREK
who so expertly chronicled the Patton story and who was
so kind in providing information for the Patton story

GUILLAUME LEMAITTE
Aviation Historian and leader of the Patton Museum
creation team in La Longeuville. He was one of the first
to volunteer for duty in the Patton aircraft recovery

Magazines

I was first contacted by the Washington, DC correspondent of Paris Match Magazine, one of the leading periodicals in France, to tell what I knew of Patton and the Scouting Force. I provided a description of the Scouting mission and names of surviving 3rd Scouting Force pilots who might have flown with Patton. A beautiful story emerged in the March 2001 issue of the magazine. *The writer had taken the few facts I had given him, along with the name of Scouts that I suggested he contact, and created a piece about the final air battle in which Patton was lost. It made exciting reading* **but it was pure fiction!**

Newspapers.

There was continuous coverage by the European press with the best writing coming from the pen of **Martine Kaczmarek** in the **La Voix du Nord** newspaper of Lille. The story was covered nationally in the US with the better stories coming from the **Kansas City Star**.

American Television Networks

The Patton story made headlines all over the world with coverage by all of the major American networks including an interview of the Patton family in Missouri by the ABC network. I am sure the European media provided equivalent coverage.

The Internet

The average Aviation Historian delves into the minutest detail with ferocity of a wounded Tiger for detail is the stuff that stories are made of. Nothing excites them more than an aircraft serial number which, when confirmed correct, is often a key element in a story. The Internet has added a new dimension as those who are experts in this are dialogue on the many Websites which feature Serial Number information. Thus the information is rapidly transmitted worldwide.

The Internet added still another opportunity for the historian and that is the ability to exchange information on a rapid basis, almost as though they were sitting in the same room chatting. Thus, many thoughts can be exchanged in a short period and the whole community can "listen" in. To the outsider, it may seem a bit weird but research is fun time for the historian. Sometimes it gets a bit wild. Such was the case with Lt. Patton's Mustang.

Initial reports from the scene of the crash identified the aircraft unearthed by the French as North American P-51D-5 NA Serial Number 44-15331. This information found its way on to the "Bulletin Board" section of a well known Mustang Website and the action began! The number was immediately challenged by one historian who was in contact with an 8th Air Force veteran who was sure that he had flown that airplane on a date later than 15 January 1945, therefore the Patton machine could not have been 15331!

It was all good fun for the participants but did not change the facts as I had received E-Mails from 3 on-the-spot French sources, confirming the correct Serial Number as 44-15331 and had, in hand, a photo of the aircraft name plate emblazoned with 44-15331, I was quite satisfied with the original reports.

The photos below leaves no doubt as to the identity of the dog tags discovered in the field on that fateful day in February 2001

Proof Positive

WHY THE DELAY IN FINDING PATTON

The Patton story should have been a short one; not a 56 year odyssey! The remains should have been located immediately, recovered and the family notified within days of the event. The decades of heartbreak should have never transpired.

Patton Mustang found the morning after the crash

Here the story takes its second tragic turn. The citizens in the village of La Longueville knew immediately of the Patton crash. It was reported to the Gendarmes in nearby Maubeuge and an investigation was launched. The Gendarmes notified American authorities and an official report, dated 16 January 1945, the day after the crash, was written by Lt. Bernard, Commandant of the Maubeuge Gendermarie and given wide distribution within the Genderme organization. The 3rd Scouting Force MIA report was issued on 18 January 1945.

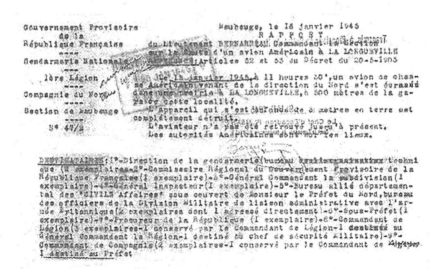

OFFICIAL REPORT OF THE PATTON CRASH BY THE GENDERMARIE AT MAUBEUGE ON 16 JANUARY

An approximate translation reads as follows:

"On 15 January 1945 at 11 hours 30 ', an American fighter coming from the direction of northeast crashed into a meadow in LONGUEVILLE within 500 meters of the railroad station been found. The American authorities have been notified."

THE CRASH WAS ALSO DOCUMENTED IN THE LOCAL FRENCH NEWSPAPER ON 17 JANUARY-2 DAYS AFTER THE CRASH

Roughly. Translated, this article reads:

"An americain plane crashed on the ground close to Avesnes on January 15, towards 11 a.m. 30 about 500 meters from the railroad station of Longueville. The plane seems lost and drives out of the fog and crashes."

The system fails

Thus, we find that there was an abundance of evidence available which should have resulted in a concentrated effort by the US Army to find Patton's airplane. The Missing Aircrew Report (MACR) filed by Patton's flight leader identified the area in which he went down, the French found the wreckage and reported it to Americans (we do not know what organization this was) and to the Gendarme chain of command plus it was reported in the local newspaper The following morning.

During World War II the United States military had an organization with the sole function of locating combat casualties, identifying them, recovering the remains and assuring proper interment. The unit was known as **Graves Registration**

History shows that Graves Registration personnel normally went to incredible lengths to do their job. One example is that of 3<u>rd Scouting Force pilot, John Stein,</u> who went missing on 6 April 1945. Stein's Individual Deceased Personnel File shows That Graves registration pursued the case for some <u>4 years </u>before the files were closed. No such action was taken in the Patton case. In fact, the Patton Graves Registration records clearly show that his case was dismissed administratively and no search was ever conducted.

Minutes of Graves Registration Review Board meetings in the Patton case, concluded that there was really no point in searching for him. From the minutes of the 7887th Graves Registration Detachment dated 7 December 1950 I quote*: "Due to <u>the absence of visual</u> evidence relative to the aircraft having crashed in the area cited, no specific field investigation could be initiated." Absence of evidence indeed!! There was no absence of evidence…just a tragic failure of communication and follow through.*

This, of course, was not the fault of this group of men. They were simply completing a chain of administrative action, set in

17

motion by a totally failed effort by the Graves Registration system. The bottom line, however, is that the Army personnel recovery apparatus failed miserably In the case of William Wyatt Patton. The result was many more victims; the entire Patton family........... For a period of 56 years.

One would think that there were lessons learned as the result of the Patton case and many similar situations after the end of World War II. On the contrary, some 78,000 American World War II MIA's still remain unaccounted for (of which 38,000 are considered recoverable) yet a minimum effort is being applied by the US Government to discover, recover and identify these fallen warriors. Most of the resources of the Joint POW/MIA Accounting Command (JPAC), the responsible agency, are directed toward the 1800 MIA's of the Southeast Asia conflict. This is somewhat understandable as next to nothing was being done about MIA's of any era until years of lobbying by families of the Southeast Asia war MIA's brought The Department of Defense to it's senses. While we now have a dedicated organization its efforts are out of balance with the overall MIA recovery need (95% of the effort going toward 5% of the MIAs), its charter is missing some key elements (JPAC has no responsibility for discovery), procedures are unnecessarily cumbersome (identification ground rules can result in years of delay) and it will not allow assistance from the public though that is how 99% of the World War II discoveries are attained. *JPAC is still the best hope for breaking the WW II MIA deadlock. Staffed by qualified and dedicated personnel, it simply operates under an incomplete charter.*

CHAPTER 2

RECOVERY OPERATIONS BEGIN

Within 2 weeks of the discovery of the Patton Mustang crash site, the recovery team had been assembled and began the difficult task of recovery. The remains were then sent to CILHI in Hawaii for positive identification

THE OFFICIAL AMERICAN RECOVERY TEAM
Once the American authorities had been notified by Gendarme Adjutant Archimbault all appropriate USAF elements were notified and movement to La Longueville began including;

US Army Central Identification Laboratory, Hawaii (CILHI)
CILHI is the US Government organization responsible for the final identification of all recovered remains of US military casualties and is located at Hickam Air Force Base on the in the state of Hawaii. Members who participated in the Patton project were:

Mr. Marc Baldwin
Major Skip Adams
Dr. Andrew Tyrell

US Army Memorial Affairs Activity-Europe

This is the US military organization in Europe, responsible for providing medical services support for operations such as the Patton project. The following personnel were involved:

Mr. David Roath
Capt. David Bundy
Dr. Katherine M. Ingwersen

OTHER AMERICAN OFFICIALS INVOLVED

American Counselate North / Pas de Calais
Katherine Koch-Counsel

American Embassy-Paris
Lt. Col. Michael Kelley
S/Sgt Gilles Spence Roserens

FRENCH OFFICIALS
Adjutant Chief Michel Archimbault –Feignies Gendermarie
Chief Robert Hannape – Maubeuge Gendermarie
Messr Patrick-First adjoint of Mayor
Messr Philipe Oustzet-Mayor adjoint

VOLUNTEER FRENCH CITIZENS
MM Cathy Archimbault-Wife of Michel
Messr Yves Dumortier-President of the Maubeuge Vintage Wings
Messr Patrick Camberlin-President-Fort Leveau Museum Association
Messr Guillaume LeMaitte-Aviation Historian
Messr Claude LeMaitte-Father of Guillaume
MM Cecile LeMaitte-Sister of Guillaume
Messr. Cedric Deroo-Aviation Historian
Messr Gilles Michelot-Aviation Historian
Messr Pierre Yves Godin-Aviation Historian

In addition to those official and volunteer persons mentioned, there were a number of local French citizens who were hired to participate in the dig and who were involved in the cleaning of the aircraft parts for identification purposes.

This is area is no stranger to war. The Germans and the French have engaged in combat for at least 1600 years, beginning with Attila the Hun in the 3rd Century and proceeding through Many tragic conflicts including the War of 1870, World War I and World War II.

The location of the crash of Pattons Mustang is in the village of La Longeuville, 6 KM west of the City of Maubeuge in the Pas de Calais area. It is located only 500 yards from the La Longueville Railroad Station. The field lies parallel to the railroad tracks between Valenciennes and Maubeuge. One of the landmarks near the Druet property is a pre-World War II Pillbox built in 1937 as a part of the defensive structure preceding the war. The ground contains a depression in the earth approximately 500 yards square at the north end of the field. Messr Druet cut 3 ditches in a north-south direction for the purpose of drainage. It was at the completion of the north end of the 3rd and eastern-most ditch that he unearthed a machine gun and ceased the operation. Messr. X cut an east-west ditch near where the gun was unearthed and found other parts of the aircraft and pilots equipment.

RECOVERY OPERATIONS

This was the focal point for the excavation and search process. The excavation of the crash site was carefully planned and executed within standard archeological Investigation procedures where possible. This was made extremely difficult by the previous unauthorized dig by Messr. X. and the movement of materials from the original location of aircraft impact.

THE DIG AREA SHOWING THE MUDDY CONDITIONS AND THE. 50 CALIBER LIVE AMMUNITION UNEARTHED

The Dig Begins

The recovery process began on 6 March 2001 with initial action assuring that the area was safe from explosive devices. An Explosive Ordnance Disposal Team cleared the field and noted that no bombs or rockets were present however, there were many live 50 caliber machine gun bullet unearthed.

The dig covered an area approximately 1200 square foot which was divided into small squares to assure the most effective search. This area was then stripped of topsoil and the detailed excavation initiated. It was an extremely difficult task because the already saturated sub-soil soil was pounded with constant rain. This resulted in very dense material to examine. The method used was to place the loads of mud on large screens and then to break it up with high pressure water hoses.

The entire area was evacuated to a depth ranging from 1 to12 feet which resulted in finding about 60% of the Mustang. This included major components such as engine, propeller, landing gear, machine guns, armor plate, aircraft structure and much of Lt. Patton's remains, his clothing and flight equipment. The recovery activity was terminated on 19 April 2001.

THE PRIME DIGGING VEHICLE

DIGGING THE CRASHSITE

THE DIG CONTINUES

A VERY MUDDY PLACE

AIRCRAFT PARTS RECOVERED

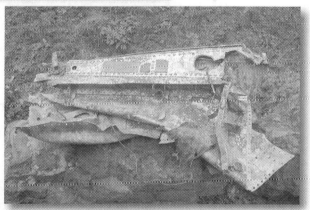

Patton Family member visits the Crash site in France

Joan Spee, daughter of Norman Taylor, Patton's Brother-in-law, was the first member of the Patton family to visit the La Longueville/ Feignies area and to view the crash site. She was hosted by Adjutant Archimbault and wife Cathy and received a wonderful and warm greeting from of the officials and citizens of the area.

**CATHY ARCHIMBAULT, JOAN SPEE
AND ADJUTANT ARCHIMBAULT**

INITIAL MILITARY HONORS ACCORDED LT. PATTON BY THE FRENCH

As the remains of Lt. Patton were found in the muddy ground, they were gently placed in a flag draped casket. Upon completion of the recovery project, with an honor guard of American and French military present the casket placed in a hearse and taken to the US Air base in Weisbaden, Germany. From there it was transported, by air, to the CILI facility in Hawaii for the final identification process.

The armed honor guard was made of French Army personnel while the Pallbearers were drawn from the ranks of the French Air Force, French Army, US Air Force and US Army personnel.

Others present included dignitaries from all of the local French communities and military dignitaries from the French and American services. The entire Patton episode represented the very best in Franco-American relations

**THE ALLIED MILITARY PAYS TRIBUTE
TO THE FALLEN WARRIOR**

THE HONORED DEAD

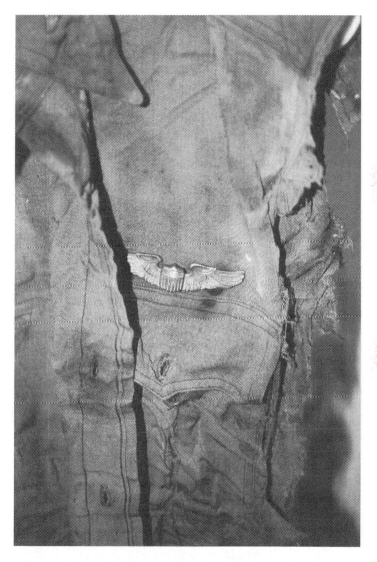

PATTON'S SHIRT
Note in good condition

CHAPTER 3

THE FINAL MISSION OF WILLIAM PATTON

The crash analysis includes examination of the misson, crash site, aircraft wreckage, pilots clothing and equipment and review of the findings of the Recovery Team

MISSION ANALYSIS

Lt Patton transferred to the 3rd Scouting Force

Lt. William Patton reported to the 3rd Scouting Force the day after checking out in the P-51 at the 55th Fighter group Clobber College. Note that his Form 5 shows his first flight as a 3rd Scout on 1 January 1945. Between the 1st and the 14th of January 1945, he made 10 flights with a total flying time of 25 hours and 30 minutes prior to the fatal mission on 15 January 1945. From this record we can conclude that Patton flew every possible hour that he was allowed. This is in keeping with Pattons character. It is apparent to me that he wanted to become proficient in the P-51 as soon as possible and to become a productive member of the 3rd Scouting Force. Because the Form 5 was not so noted, we do not know which of these flights were mission training, bomber formation assistance or scouting missions.

Final Mission

The Kodak White flight, led by Lt. Bryan Booker, with William Patton as his wingman, originated at Wormingford Airfield near Colchester, England. Their mission was to notify the 3rd Air Division Leader of the weather conditions over the English Channel and into Eastern France. This placed them on a course of approximately 133 degrees to Metz, France where they turned to return home. However, instead of setting a course for Wormingford, Booker chose to head for Lille, letting down into a bank of fog which stretched from 1200 feet to the ground. The entry in Patton's Form 5 for the 15th of January was 2 hours. We can assume that Lt. Booker reported this to the 3SF Operations NCO when he returned to Wormingford. In analyzing the final mission, this figure was used for the flight from Wormingford to 06 Degrees East Longitude and return to the point of the crash at La Longeuville.

AS PATTON'S MUSTANG MAY HAVE LOOKED

INDIVIDUAL FLIGHT RECORD

(1) SERIAL NO. O-758480 (2) NAME PATTON WILLIAM B., JR. (3) RANK 1st Lieut. (3A) A/C 1913
(5) PERS. CLASS. 1B (6) BRANCH Army Air Forces (7) STATION AAF Station F-150
(8) ORGANIZATION ASSIGNED 8th 3rd Div 45th 388th 580th
(9) ORGANIZATION ATTACHED 8th 3rd Div 3rd Scouting Force
(10) PRESENT RATING & DATE Pilot - 5/11/43 (11) ORIGINAL RATING & DATE P - 5/11/43
(12) TRANSFERRED FROM (13) FLIGHT RESTRICTIONS None
(13) TRANSFERRED TO (14) TRANSFER DATE

(17) MONTH January 1945

DAY	AIRCRAFT TYPE, MODEL & SERIES			COMD PILOT	CO-PILOT		FIRST PILOT DAY / NIGHT		RATED PERS. NON-PILOT	NON-RATED				SPECIAL INFORMATION			
									P-51								
1	P-51D	1					1:45										
2	P-51D	1					2:40										
3	P-51D	1					2:10										
4	P-51D	1					3:10										
5	P-51D	1					3:00										
7	P-51D	1					3:25										
8	P-51D	1					2:50										
8	P-51D	1					1:50										
14	P-51D	1					3:00										
14	P-51D	1					2:00										
15	P-51D	1					2:00										

"CERTIFIED CORRECT"

STANLEY K. GAGON,
Major, Air Corps,
Operations Officer.

COLUMN TOTALS				27:30										
		(18) TOTAL STUDENT PILOT TIME			(19) TOTAL FIRST PILOT TIME			(20) TOTAL PILOT TIME		
(12) THIS MONTH				27:30	0:00	27:30	0:00
(13) PREVIOUS MONTHS THIS F.Y.				50:15	0:00	51:45	0:00
(13) THIS FISCAL YEAR				77:45	0:00	79:15	0:00
(14) PREVIOUS FISCAL YEARS	273:55			213:30	26:10	629:55	0:00
(15) TO DATE	273:55			291:15	26:10	709:10	0:00

Lt. Bryan J. Booker Jr.

Lt. Booker was the flight leader on the ill fated mission which took the life of Lt. William W. Patton.

The Summary section of the mission included in the Missing Aircrew Report is shown below

Lt. Booker was killed in an accident a few days later while returning from a mission over Germany.

" 12 January 1948

Stanley E. Gagm

STANLEY E. GAGM,
Major, AC., Operations Officer.

Because lost pilot made no indication that his radio was out,
leader presumed that he heard the R/T message to make a 180
to the left. Aircraft started turn in trail of leader, and
was out of sight of leader during turn. Leader was not forced
to go on instruments, but it is presumed that #2 man got into
instrument conditions on outside of turn and went on instruments
without realizing that he was in a turn. No visual evidence of
crash in area (from the air), but no further radio contact seems
to indicate that lost aircraft crashed after going on instruments.

Bryan J. Booker, Jr.

BRYAN J. BOOKER, JR.,
1st Lieut., Air Corps,
O-781772.

LT. BOOKER'S STATEMENT

WAR DEPARTMENT
HEADQUARTERS ARMY AIR FORCES
WASHINGTON

MISSING AIR CREW REPORT

	Wormingford	Eighth Air Force
		3rd Air Division
388th B.G.	560th B.S.	DS to 3rd. Scouting Force
	Wormingford	388
	Lechfeld	Weather Scouting

Strato Cumulus cloud at 1500' and ground fog at 1200'.
15 JAN '45   1115   Roubaix, France

While making 180 degree turn in fog, while separated
from leader, believed to have spun-in.

P51D15NA   44-15331
(None)
V-1650-7

Number (1) V-326583

Buffalo Arms-.50-1301393	(3)	Colt-.50-1032041	
Buffalo Arms-.50-1301158	(3)	Buffalo Arms-.50-1301406	
Buffalo Arms-.50-1299119	(3)	Buffalo Arms-.50-1600786	
			X
1 Passengers			1

Crew Position
1. Pilot   Patton, William W., Jr. 1/Lt O-758480   Pilot

2. Bryan J. Booker   1/Lt O-751721   X

Other Mission Possibilities

While the 15 January flight is the only confirmed mission that Patton flew, it is probable that he did participate in missions on the 2nd, 4th, 5th, 7th, and 14th of January 1945 and could have been on the "bomber herding" activities of the 1st, 3rd, and 8th of January. This is based upon the known flight hours logged by other 3rd Scouting Force pilots during the first 2 weeks of January 1945. The following chart shows these comparisons.

DATE	TARGET	FLIGHT HOURS LOGGED			
		Patton	Lancaster	Abendroth	Klasinski
1st	Dollbergen	1:45	2:30	5:25	5:20
2 nd	Bad Kreuznach	2:45	***	3:00	4:10
3rd	Fulda	2:10	***	4:15	4:15
4th	Local Flying	3:10	***	***	***
5th	H a n a u - Frankfurt	3:00	3:00	3:15	***
7th	Bielfield	3:25	3:30	***	3:35
8th	Bischofshein	2:30 / 1:50	3:00	3:10	***
10th	Karlsruhe	***	3:45	***	***
13th	Mainz	***	3:40	***	3:40
14th	Derber	3:00 / 2:00	3:05	***	4:35
15th	Augsburg	2:00	***	***	5:00

CONFIRMED JANUARY 1945 MISSIONS BY 3SF PILOTS

Capt. Orvid Lancaster

Lt. Luverne Abendroth

Lt. Tony Klasinski

8ᵀᴴ AIR FORCE MISSION SUMMARY

Field Order 8AF 794 directed the 1ˢᵗ, 2ⁿᵈ and 3ʳᵈ Air Division to bomb the Munich area on Monday 15 January 1945. Primary Target of the 3ʳᵈ Division was the Messerschmitt Aircraft Factory at Augsburg but it was completely obscured by clouds so the decision was made to go to the secondary target which was the Marshalling Yards at Augsburg. 253 of the B-17 Force hit this Secondary Target hard. The balance of 34 Fortresses hit Targets Of Opportunity in the Munich area.

3ᴿᴰ SCOUTING FORCE MISSION SUMMARY

Based upon the 15 January 1945 3ʳᵈ Scouting Force Mission Summary as, provided by the USAF History Office, the following activity transpired: The 3ʳᵈ Scouting Force launched a maximum effort of 13 aircraft in support of the 3ʳᵈ Division bomber force deployed as follows:

"13 P-51 aircraft airborne between 0905 and 0955. 12 aircraft landed safely this base between 1210 and 1553. Remaining aircraft believed to have landed on continent in the vicinity of Lille.

A. 2 aircraft call sign Kodak Control (also referred to as Koday Yellow) assisted division leader in assembly. All wings in good formation.

B. 2 aircraft call sign Kodak White flew bomber route to 060 degrees east reporting low fog over bases; 10/10's over channel (at) 7-8000 feet, high cloud near Charleroi (at) 20-23000 feet with fair visibility. CAVU to Metz, fog in all valleys. Division in good formation with exception of one group out at the side. Contacts were made at CPL1 with Vampire (45ᵗʰ Combat Wing), who relayed to Clambake (93ʳᵈ Combat Wing) and Hotshot (4ᵗʰ Combat Wing) Vampire contacted at Charleroi and all group leaders at Metz.

A. 8 aircraft plus one spare call sign Kodak Red, flew to target area arriving and reporting bombing time minus 37 minutes. target area no high, no middle, 10/10's low stratus reported to Vampire who relayed to Clambake and Hotshot. Bombs away at 1229 and were seen to cover a large area. Formation good throughout IP to RP. Light meager flak seen in target area. communications good with leaders. Rocket seen at 1048 from Koln area."

Missing Air Crew Report (MACR) number 11919, dated 18 January 2001

The time of Patton's disappearance was 1115 hours and Patton's form 5 shows 2 hours flying time. That would put takeoff at 0915 hours. The accident took place near La Longueville France, about 160 air miles from the 3SF base at Wormingford, England and about 35 miles Southeast of the Lille/Roubaix area. The pair were on a heading of 325 degrees with weather conditions reported by Booker as Strato Cumulus clouds at 1500 foot altitude and ground fog at 1200 feet above the terrain.

Lt. Booker states in Section 5 of the MACR: *"While making 180 turn in the fog, while separated from the leader, believed to have spun-in"*

He further states in Section 17 : *"because lost pilot (Patton) made no indication that his radio was out, leader(Booker) presumed that he heard the R/T(radio transmission) message to make a 180 degree (turn) to the left. Aircraft started turn in trail of the leader and was out of sight of the leader during the turn. Leader was not forced to go on instruments, but it is presumed that #2 man got in instrument conditions outside of the turn and went on instruments without realizing that he was in a turn. No visual evidence of crash in the area (from the air), but no further radio contacts seems to indicate that lost aircraft crashed after going on instrument."*

This represents the total information available, from the military side. This MACR was filed on 18 January by Lt. Bryan J.Booker Jr. and signed by Major Stanley E. Gagon, 3rd Scouting Force Operations Officer.

MAJOR STANLEY GAGON
EXECUTIVE OFFICER
3RD SCOUTING FORCE

From the Mission Summary and the MACR we have prepared the following drawing of the flight path, determined critical checkpoints and are able develop an accident scenario.

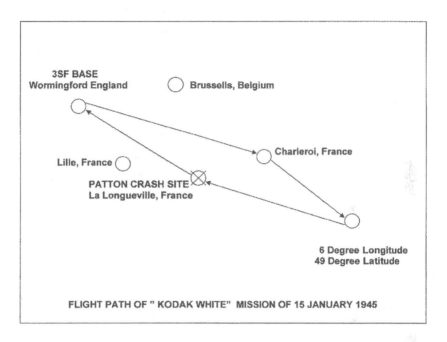

3SF BASE
Wormingford England

Brussels, Belgium

Charleroi, France

Lille, France

PATTON CRASH SITE
La Longueville, France

6 Degree Longitude
49 Degree Latitude

FLIGHT PATH OF " KODAK WHITE" MISSION OF 15 JANUARY 1945

Data available upon discovery of the aircraft on 22 February 2001 and subsequent investigation by the US Air Force investigation team adds some to the story. The photographs of the aircraft wreckage indicate that his North American P-51-15NA Serial Number 44-15331 hit in a near flat attitude and was not destroyed in the accident as would have been the case if the aircraft dove into the ground. This is very obvious when looking at the propeller, which is essentially intact with blades bent in a forward direction. The condition of the wing guns indicates that it hit one wing first, bending the guns from outboard to inboard with decreasing degrees of damage. The left hand landing gear was also bent as the result of the left wing hitting first. The other bit of evidence supporting the flat impact is the propeller nose cone which incurred only moderate damage to the front, lower section. Lack of damage to engine also supports this contention. I believe that the majority of damage to the airframe was caused by the machinery used by Monsieur X.

The Aircraft wreckage

The aircraft was recovered in a number of large pieces plus many small parts and fragments. Confirming crash damage is difficult because of the initial unearthing which was accomplished with a backhoe without regard for any archeological considerations. There is, however, very clear evidence that can support, with reasonable accuracy, reconstruction of the accident. The following is an assessment of those parts.

Tail section-Local citizens reported to Patton family member Joan Spee, that the tail of Pattons Mustang protruded above the soil surface for some time after the crash. It was then removed for scrap metal value or as a souvenir.

Engine and Propeller-The largest portion of the aircraft recovered was the engine, with propeller attached and **the blades were bent forward. Spinner was lightly dented on bottom.**

Landing gear -The left hand landing gear is bent well forward, while the right hand gear appears to be straight. This supports the left wing down, left turn assumption. Whether gear was up or down Was not investigated

Machine Guns-Three of the machine gun barrels are bent in varying degrees. These were obviously the left hand guns

Oxygen Bottle-One Oxygen bottle undamaged, the other badly damaged. These are located side by side in the aircraft.

Radiators-Damage to the coolant and oil radiators was moderate, adding further credence to the assumption that the airplane struck the ground in a flat attitude and that the surface was moderately soft.

Clothing and Personal Equipment

The shirt was in amazingly good condition with the primary damage being the missing right sleeve. Given the condition of the shirt it can be safely assumed that the sleeve was destroyed when Messr-X made the unauthorized passes with his backhoe. <u>Tie and scarf</u> were totally intact and in good condition. <u>B-10 Jacket</u> was pretty badly mangled and about 40% of the material was missing. **The** <u>Life Jacket</u> was completely intact and in good condition except for what appears to be fire damage<u>.</u> Only a small portion of the **boots** were recovered and they were in bad condition. Only a small portion of the <u>cloth helmet</u> was recovered.

Insignia was still pinned to the shirt, pilot wings were in perfect shape, the wing & propeller insignia was in good condition, except for a slight bending of the lower portion of the propeller, and the first Lieutenant bar was undamaged

The parachute canopy and shroud lines were intact and in amazingly good condition

Shirt

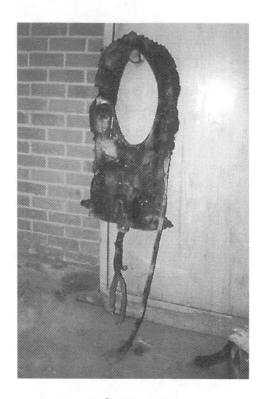

Life Preserver

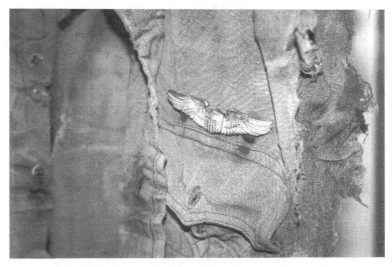

Pilot's Silver Wings

PERSONAL ITEMS RECOVERED

The government issue A-11 wrist watch was recovered
some 5 years after the aircraft wreckage search
was completed. It is a story not yet finished.

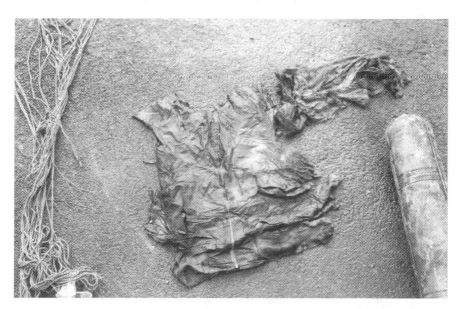

Pilot Flight Coveralls

Scarf and Tie

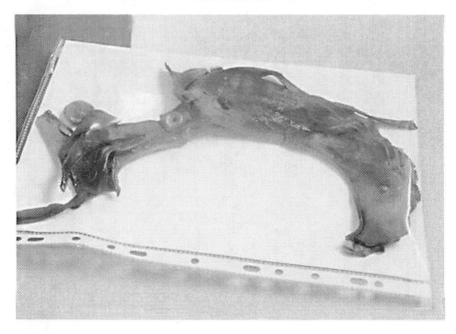

Portion of Cloth Helmet

PERSONAL ITEMS RECOVERED

OXYGEN BOTTLE- NOTE LACK OF SERIOUS DAMAGE

AIRCRAFT MACHINE GUNS
ONLY 5 OF THE 6 GUNS RECOVERED

ACCIDENT THEORY

My theory of the crash sequence has Patton going into the overcast and just as he starts the turn, developing vertigo and immediately losing control, entering a spin with the final portion of the spin slamming the aircraft into the swampy ground in a near flat attitude. This scenario is probable because of the of the peculiar spin characteristics of the P-51. They are described in AAF P-51D FLIGHT MANUAL AN 01-60JE-151 MUSTANG. Paragraph 16 (1). b. it reads"…..to start a spin the airplane snaps ½ turn in the direction of the spin with the nose dropping to near vertical. **At the end of one turn the nose rises to or above above the horizon and the spin slows down, occasionally coming almost to a complete stop. ……….**

Booker noted in the MACR that he had called for a 180 turn to the left (assuming he was letting down to land at lille, France). In the Patton scenario Loss of control happened during the left hand turn so it can be assumed that the airplane spun to the left and started with power-on. This is also confirmed by wing damage. Because Patton's prop blades were bent, it can also be assumed that the engine was running when the airplane hit the ground. With all blades bent aft it could indicate some aft movement on impact but dear riend and seasoned FAA investigator Fred Maupin of warbird and other prop driven aircraft crash studies, indicated that this was not necessarily true.

In summary, the airplane was 10 to 20 degrees nose high with the left wing down, spinning to the left, engine running and struck the ground tail first, with moderate aft velocity and a vertical velocity of approximately 100 to 150 Feet per second. This hypothesis of the accident dynamics was reviewed with a high-time Mustang pilot, Mr. Lou Lauderback, who has performed over 400 intentional spins in the Mustang. He agreed with my initial theory and pointed out that about 1300 feet of altitude would be lost in a single turn under the conditions described. Mr. Lauderback also provided video tape, taken during a spin test, which was from a camera mounted on a P-51 airframe. Analysis of this tape further supports my assessment of the flight dynamics

Another theory that could be applied, in lieu of or attendant to the vertigo theory, is that of fuel in the 75 gallon fuselage tank. Located just aft of the pilot, this his fuel provides additional range which is critical on long missions. However, this additional weight of almost 500 pounds, is in a position to cause a shift the CG (center-of-gravity) aft to a degree which adversely affects the flight characteristics of the aircraft. Sharp movements of the flight controls can easily cause the Mustang to enter a power-on spin. The standard mission procedure is to burn the fuselage fuel first to avoid being caught in a combat situation with an airplane that easily spins.

THE BIG QUESTIONS

A number of questions come to mind: with the first being, what was their mission? speeds for various missions flown ranged from about 200 to 240 miles per hour. It would seem most likely Booker and Patton were Kodak White, as noted above, and after finishing the assembly task, Booker decided to go on into France for some sightseeing or R&R.

Pattons clothing and personal equipment recovered at the site may provide additional insight for this analysis. The first clue is his attire which was not unique for a combat mission but would certainly fit with a planned visit to the big city. Rather than being clad in a flying suit, he was wearing a Class-B dress uniform. The dress green shirt, complete with pilots wings and lieutenants bars was in excellent condition and accompanied by a dress tie. Though the trousers were not found, dress pinks or greens would complete the uniform. This is the uniform that an AAF officer wore as working attire and for informal social occasions. This is possibly an indication to me that the pair might have planned on landing for a little R&R after completion of their bomber assembly work. For warmth, Patton wore the fur lined, fur collared, cloth body, AAF B-10 jacket.

Brussels, Belgium and Lille, France would be ideal places for some rest and relaxation. Colonel Ed Beaty, USAF (Ret) who was the 3rd Scouting Force Operations Officer at the time of Patton's crash, told me that it was not unusual for the Kodak Yellow or White(called Kodak Control in the mission report), as the assembly assistance Mustangs were named, to accompany the bombers to the French coast in completion of their task.

If this was the case then they would have been only about 80 air miles from the accident site when they left the bombers. As Kodak White, they were only 30 minutes from Brussels when they left the bomber stream.

The bigger question is why did Booker take Patton into an instrument situation and why was Patton in trail rather than flying on Bookers wing. One sad fact that emerged from the war in Europe was that as many pilots were lost in operational accidents and training as were lost in combat and that flying in instrument conditions was the chief cause of non-combat fatalities in fighter aircraft. In fact, that was the confirmed or suspected cause of at least 50 Percent of Scout fatalities in the three Scouting Forces. Although a qualified instrument pilot in the B-17, *Patton had ZERO instrument time in the P-51.* He had logged only 10 hours of B-17 Actual Instrument time while in Europe and that was on 2 flights in May 1944 while with the 94th Bomb Group. Flying instruments in a P-51 is infinitely more risky than in the B-17 because bombers respond rather slowly to any situation while fighters can get in trouble very quickly.

My first impression when reading the MACR was that it started in the middle of the story. I would have expected some words about the mission itself. For my way of thinking, it was too terse and indicated concern on the part of Lt. Booker. There is no question that he would have been emotionally disturbed by the event, as would any leader who whose charge was killed following their leaders words and actions. I believe the bottom line is that they were headed for Brussels or Lille to land for an unauthorized R & R (Rest and Relaxation) stop and that

Booker misjudged both the weather conditions and Patton's instrument flying capability. This was definitely a no-no but it was not uncommon for a pilot to declare that he had a rough running engine or some other aircraft malfunction and had to land immediately. We will never know for sure because both pilots are deceased, but this seems to be a most plausible theory.

PART II

YOUNG WILLIAM PATTON

WHO WAS WILLIAM PATTON

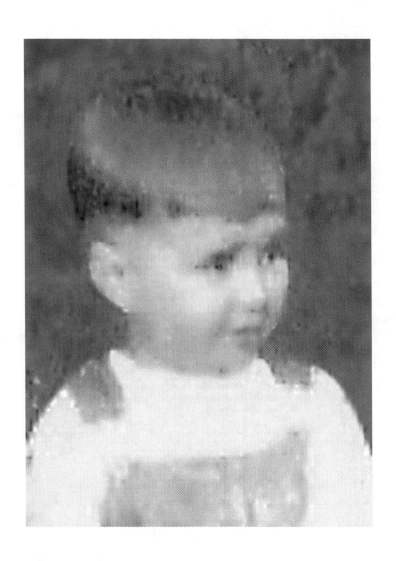

CHAPTER 4

THE PATTON FAMILY

We locate the present day Patton heirs in Neosho Missouri and, in addition to finding as treasure trove Of information about our hero, marvelous relationship was established between our two families

WE MEET THE PATTONS

Our very first contact with the Patton family came shortly after I discovered that William Patton was indeed, a member of the Scouting Force. The press coverage was extensive and through that I found that Neosho, Missouri was the home of the Patton family. An Internet search revealed the name of Angela Brown Vogel, Who is in the real estate business there. I contacted her and communication was established.

Upon establishing contact, wife Marian and I were invited to Neosho to meet the family and on 1 May 2001 we had the pleasure of spending the day with a sweet group of Patton ladies. We met at the home of Margaret Patton, widow of Wendell Patton, who was William Patton Junior's brother. In addition to Margaret attendees included: Donna Patton Brown and Joyce Patton Montez, daughters of Wendell & Margaret Patton and Connie Patton, daughter of Keith & Pauline Patton. What a great time we had talking about "Junior," the family name for William Patton Junior.

After a bit of conversation and fine cup of coffee, Connie Patton revealed a large cardboard box which was filled with documents, photographs and artifacts which had belonged to William Jr. during his lifetime. Connie, who had purchased the family home after the death of Williams parents, found the box in the attic along with military uniform items. Needless to say I was surprised and overjoyed at so much material about him was available. I began to examine each item and thus began a bond with William Wyatt Patton Jr. which shall remain with me for the rest of my life. It was at that point that I volunteered to write "Juniors" biography. The family immediately accepted.

As I poured over this material, the conversation became even more animated and I felt that closure for the family was finally beginning after the many decades since William's death. It was a great day that ended all too soon.

We had another great visit to Neosho in July 2001 and gathered additional material for Junior's biography. Had the pleasure of meeting many other members of the family, enjoying a great Barbeque Lunch and having another great time. The spirit of Junior Patton filled the air to make this an even more enjoyable occasion.

AUTHOR DICK ATKINS AND COUSIN CONNIE PATTON REVIEW WILLIAM PATTON DOCUMENTS

Connie Patton, Joyce Patton Montez, Donna Patton Brown and Margaret Patton

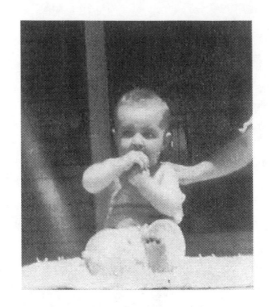

LITTLE WILLIAM PATTON

WILLIAM ALL GROWN UP

**SIBLINGS KEITH, BILLIE AND WENDELL PATTON
WITH PARENTS WILLIAM SR. AND RHODA PATTON**

THE PATTON FAMILY GENEALOGY

The Patton family, as this story unfolds, begins with Junior's parents, William Wyatt Patton Senior and Rhoda Gold Patton. A document was found that confirmed the beginning of the Patton clan. It was written by Junior's Mother, Rhoda.

> *"On the 9th day of August 1914 Wyatt Patton drove horse and buggy to the home of Rhoda Gold. We went to the home of Rev Boyd Phillips. He performed the marriage ceremony. Witnesses were Maymie Phillips and Albert Phillips. We then went to Springs Oklahoma to make our home. Wyatt had a job at Costens Oil Refinery in Tulsa. William Wyatt Patton Junior was born on 10 January 1918. These were good times for our family but the togetherness was soon to end with the entry of the United States into World War I.*

> *We lived in Oklahoma until Wyatt went into the Service (Army). We moved back to Neosho, Missouri where William and I moved in with Rhoda's Parents. William Senior left Neosho on the 21st of June 1918 for Camp Pike, Arkansas. He was shipped out of Camp Pike on 23 August 1918 and then on to France. There was no communication with Wyatt for an extensive period after his departure. This was an excruciating period for me, not knowing the whereabouts of my husband. Finally, 3 months after his departure communications was resumed. He was safe! It was to be long wait for William Sr. He did not return home until the Spring of 1920".*

The Children of William Wyatt Patton Sr. and wife Rhoda

- Son William Wyatt Jr. was never married.
- Son Wendell married Margaret Lois Prather. They had 4 children: Donna, Joyce, Debbie and Sharon. Donna is Mrs. William Brown, Joyce is Mrs. Benjamin Montez, Debbie is Mrs. Rick Vogt and Sharon Patton is Mrs. Mike Cochran

- Son Keith married Pauline Kimbrough. Their children included Darrell, William and Connie
- Daughter Billie Jean married Norman Taylor. This union produced 2 children; daughter Joan and son Mike. Joan is Mrs. Harry Spee and Mike is single

WILLIAM WYATT PATTON JUNIOR

William Wyatt Patton, known as Junior by family and friends, was a typical lad of this era in terms of his day to day activities and friends. He attended school in Stark City, fished, hunted and participated in all of the other games and mischief that young boys are fond of. He was a typical child of Great Depression. But his ambition was quite different from his contemporaries; he dreamed of joining the Army Air Corp. The features that set him apart from his schoolmates was his tremendous personality, intelligence, commitment and his burning desire to enter the military. These attributes are evident throughout his short life and the following words of his contemporaries bear dramatic witness to these facts! Early research and discussions with family members led me to believe that "Junior" Patton was enamored with the thought of military service in his teens or earlier. This was confirmed in an interview with his cousin, Ross Langley,. Langley was Patton's idol and mentor. The boys were inseparable until Langley left for military service, thereby opening the path that Patton would follow.

AUTHORS NOTE: In the "It's a Small World" Department, conversation between Ross Langley and myself revealed that he and I were stationed at Randolph Air Force Base at the same time and probably crossed paths. He was in the Athletic Department and I was a Student in Flight School.

From Cousin Ross Langley

"I met Junior shortly after his birth in January 1918. His mother and father accompanied Junior to visit our home in Stark City, Missouri.

His Father was my mother's younger brother and destined for shipment to France for fighting in World War I.

Shortly after Junior's birth an electric storm killed both of my parents and I went to live with our Patton grandparents in Gravette, Arkansas. Soon thereafter Junior and his mother moved into the Grandparents household and remained several months until Juniors father returned from overseas They lived in Gravette for about 6 months before moving to a farm directly across the road from our Grandfathers farm near Stark City, Missouri.

I was shipped to Missouri to live with a relative and work on their farms, all within a mile of each other. After 4 years of living at Gravette, Arkansas our grandparents became disenchanted with others farming his old homestead so we moved back across the road from Juniors family. I remained with our grandparents for another 6 years before enlisting in the US Army.

In 1931 I was assigned to the Army Air Corps at Randolph Field (in San Antonio, Texas). I frequently visited my Missouri relatives, especially Junior and his family/ When Junior was 14 years old he began to show interest in a military career. At the time I discouraged him saying, no help from me until he graduated from high school. I would drive up and talk his family into giving their blessing and assist him to enlist.

Instead of writing me that he was ready for the military, on Sunday morning following his Friday graduation, he showed up on my barracks porch at Randolph both dirty and hungry. I cleaned him up and fed him. Next morning we went to the Recruiting Office and discovered he was underweight and could not enlist. There were no waivers for underweight. I told him to cheer up, I could fix that in a week. I talked our Mess Sergeant into giving him a job in the Mess Hall as a Table Waiter while living in my barracks and eating lots of bananas. In less than a week he had gained sufficient weight to enlist.

**COUSIN COLONEL ROSS LANGLEY
WILLIAM'S MENTOR**

**BROTHER-IN-LAW NORMAN TAYLOR WITH
WILLIAM PATTONS PORTRAIT**

SISTER-IN-LAW MARGARET PATTON

during the first six weeks of Junior's military life he exhibited the most reserved, polite and timid character I have ever observed. Within two months personality had blossomed into friendliness, cheerfulness and respect for others. We served together in the headquarter squadron for more than six years. He known as And the military became the most likable and respected member of our squadron. For When World War II military expansion began in 1940 I was assigned to Moffett Field near San Jose California and genuine worship the Pearl Harbor Hawaii he survived the attack on Pearl Harbor and became a bomber crew member participating in the battle of Midway.

In March 1942, as a member of the West Coast training command, we moved to Santa Ana California. About six months later, at 2 AM, I was awakened by ringing and pounding on the apartment door. Junior had returned as a master sergeant to undergo preflight training Santa Ana air base. Fortunately, this is cousin slightly privileged, I managed to take him home with me every weekend during his training. Then with some of his old friends and personnel we managed to sign him to our primary and basic flight training at nearby Ontario California. We still managed to bring them home with us most weekends. When Junior finishes primary training I was assigned to the initial B-29 command headquarters destine for India, China and the Marianas.

For My wife and I dearly love Pat, more like a brother than a cousin. At age 93 yes still deeply grieve over the loss of Pat. Hopefully you will be able to get a picture of Pat's younger, eventful years as well as his short life in the military."

From Sister-in-law Margaret Patton

"I remember visiting with Mom and Dad Patton while Junior was in the service, they were always anxiously waiting for the mail, hoping that they would hear from Junior. Wendell was quite young when Junior left home and really said very little about their home life. We always felt that Junior would be coming home one day."

From Niece Joyce Patton Montez

"Junior started school at Diamond Hall, Missouri in a one room schoolhouse approximately 5 miles from his home. He was quickly advanced to the 3rd grade as he was an excellent and intelligent student. Classmates **John and Shirley Barnes** *recall Junior being the same age as John but being 2 or 3 grades*

PATTON AND
BORDEN PETERSON

ahead of John. Classmate **David Weems** *remembers how Junior always talked about joining the Army. This was his life ambition, his dream. He remembered how Junior and his friend,* **Borden Peterson,** *would stand tall with their backs straight and march the halls of Midway High School, pretending to be Army soldiers."*

Nephew William Gary Patton remembers

"I am a native of Neosho (Newton County) Missouri. I spent many of my early years with my paternal grandparents, Wyatt and Rhonda Patton. My father, Loren Keith Patton was on the road with the Railway Express Agency. My mother, Pauline Kimbrough Patton, was ill for my months and during that period, my grandparents raised me. I have many fond memories of this time on the farm. During this time of my life I began to learn of my uncle, known to the family as Junior. Though I must confess, I thought it strange that no one wanted to speak in detail about him. I learned later in my life of the pain that my grandparents felt when he was lost.

A little about myself and my family: I am married to Virginia Anise of Biloxi, Mississippi who was born at Kessler Air Force Base. Her father was a career officer in the Air Force. We were married in Feb. 1971 in Marshall, TX. We have two sons, William Gary Patton, Jr. of Bossier City, LA and Robert Wyatt Patton, Sr. of Hallsville, TX. Gary, Jr. is married to Lisa Kazuba and they have one son William Gary Patton, III. Robby is married to Betty Chandler and they have four children, Robert Wyatt Patton, Jr., Jathon Charles, and the twins Alayna and Adrianna. I am a veteran of the Vietnam Conflict. I served with the 6th Bn. 14th Artillery Reg. We were the "Big Guns of the Central Highlands" consisting of four firing batteries of 8" and 175mm howitzers. I served in country from July 1969-June 1970. My total military service lasted six years and I promoted to the rank of staff sergeant. I currently live in Shreveport, LA and am employed as a supervisor with the Louisiana Dept. of Social Services. Retirement is not to far away. Most of my time is spent with my grand children and family

I have many memories of growing up in the shadow of William Wyatt Patton, Jr. He was a family icon and his is a very sad story. I can remember Grandma Rhonda sometimes crying when I would ask her to tell me about him. I have always felt a deep, strong connection to him. This is partly due to being named after him, at least the name William. My mother and father argued about naming me (stories told later in life) after Junior. My dad wanted me to be William Wyatt number III, but my mother would not have any part of it. As a result, they compromised.

Periodically through out my life my Grandma Rhoda would sometimes slip and call be Junior and she did treat me like I was a son. I can recall when grandma saved up enough money to have a marker made for Junior to be placed at the National Military Park in Springfield, MO. This provided her with some closure. When we returned on day from visiting the park she let me look at the medals that he had received during his service. She was very proud of his sacrifice, but the "not knowing" what had happened to him troubled her all of her life.

Grandpa never spoke of Junior that I can recall. He would only answer questions I had with very brief responses and then change the subject. He too felt the incredible pain, but being stoic, refused to show any emotion, at least not in front of me. My father would tell stories of them as boys growing up on the farm, but even he would not go very far with the story, relating only basic facts. " One story my dad liked to tell involved a watermelon Junior and Wendell had placed in a spring to chill so they could eat it when they finished working in the fields that day. Dad and a friend crept up to the spring and took the watermelon, cut it open and began to eat it. They had not eaten much when Junior and Wendell came for "their" melon only to find

Then chase was on. My dad said he could out run both Junior and Wendell so he was never caught. The older brothers finally tired of chasing little brother and returned to the, now not so cold, watermelon. The following summer, Junior graduated from high school and made his way to Randolph Field, TX and began his military career. This is the only story I can recall that was ever told by my dad about his older brother. After grandpa died in '74 and grandma died in '89 the families went their own way with very little contact until Junior was recovered.

I learned about his P-51 being discovered in France while driving to pick up my grandsons on a Monday evening. I was listening to the Nightly News with Tom Brokow when I heard that the body of a WW II pilot had been recovered in France. I was stunned when I heard the pilot's name, William Patton. I returned home that evening and called my sister Connie in Newton County, MO. I related my experience and she confirmed that the plane had in fact been found with the pilot sitting in the cockpit. All evidence supported that this was in fact William Wyatt Patton, Jr. of Stark City, MO. I told Connie that I would call the local NBC affiliate and see if I could get a copy of the video tape. The next morning I called the local NBC station and was informed that the video was the property of NBC and I could contact New York to see about a copy. Of course I made the call stating that I was Gary Patton and would like a copy of the video. I was told to expect a call back in a few minutes, but of course no call came.

I then called back and stated that my name was William Patton and I was interested in more information about the MIA that had been located in France. About ten minutes later I received a call back from the producer of The Nightly News w/ Tom Brokow. The lady I spoke with was very interested in my connection to the pilot and I told her that I felt he might be my uncle who had been missing for 56 years and I just wanted a copy of the video for the family, as well as any other information the news agency might have about the recovery. I was then told to expect a call back from her with details about getting a copy of the video. Approximately 15 minutes after this conversation I received a phone call from London. This call was from the producer of the original story. She indicated from the evidence at the scene that the pilot was in fact, my uncle. Of course much more had to be done to confirm this. I terminated that call only to get a call from New York. Brokow's producer wanted to pursue the story. She wanted family in Newton County, as opposed to me in Louisiana. I called my cousin Joyce to see if she would speak with the news people, she adamantly refused. So, I called my sister Connie and she agreed to be the family spokesman and the rest is history."

I will close with one final story that impacted me tremendously. During the time of Junior's funeral in Neosho, I was living in Bienville Parish, Louisiana about 60 miles southeast of Shreveport. The day we returned home I was standing on my boat dock and noticed a WW II vintage aircraft doing loops directly over the house. I had never seen this before at the lake nor did I see it again. I felt like it was a sign from Junior that he appreciated what the family had done and that I was no longer in the shadow of him. I know it was coincidence, but also a great irony."

While the Missing–In-Action message was the initial tragedy, there were many more chapters of family suffering. Two generations of Pattons, closest to 'Junior,' went to their graves not knowing the final answer. Mother and Father Patton, brother Keith and wife Pauline, brother Wendell, and sister Billie all died without knowing Juniors fate. The rest of the family waited 56 years for the answer.

TODDLER WILLIAM WYATT PATTON JR.

**BOTHERS WENDELL AND WILLIAM
PATTON AND POOCH**

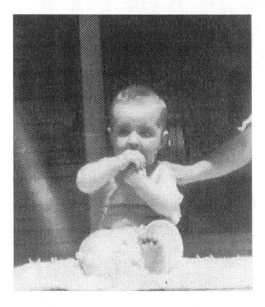

INFANT WILLIAM PATTON – CUTE KID

**COUSIN JOAN (TAYLOR) SPEE AND
GRANDMA RHODA PATTON**

COUSIN GLADWYN GOLD AND WILLIAM PATTON

PATTON FAMILY PHOTOS

A number of photographs were provided to the author by the Patton family with many of the subjects identified however, there are some of the older ones, especially the ones with large groups, that are listed only as "Patton family."

THE PATTON KIDS-PROBABLY IN THE MID 20'S

SENIOR PATTONS GATHER

FAMILY REUNION

FAMILY GATHERINGS OVER THE YEARS

THE PATTON HOMESTEAD

**PRIVATE FIRST CLASS WILLIAM
WYATT PATTON JR -1937
"JUNIOR" PATTON
NEW ARMY AIR CORPS RECRUIT
1934**

CHAPTER 5

EARLY MILITARY SERVICE

It was obvious from an early age that Junior Patton was destined for a military career and from the very beginning of that adventure he was a superior soldier and airman

INTO THE AIR CORPS AT RANDOLPH FIELD, SAN ANTONIO, TEXAS

One can imagine Patton's excitement when he first viewed Cousin Ross Langley's military uniform during Patton's High School tenure. Langley states that Patton wanted to quit school and enlist but was admonished by his idol to stay and graduate from High School, which he did in April 1934. Immediately after graduation, according to Langley, Patton packed his bags and hitchhiked to San Antonio, Texas to visit with his cherished friend and to enlist in the Army Air Corps. Unfortunately, Patton could not pass his initial physical exam because he was underweight. Heartbroken, he went to Langley for consolation. Being a practical man who wanted to see his young charge realize his dreams, Ross devised a plan to fatten young Patton. Ross arranged Aa job for Patton in the Base Mess Hall as a civilian employee and supervised a crash course of weight enhancing foods. A steady diet of bananas was a major contributor in reaching enlistment weight. The objective was accomplished and *at the tender age of **16 years–5*** *months–17 days*, on 26 June 1934, Patton became a member of the US Army Air Corps. His dream was realized.

After completing basic training at Randolph, he entered Aircraft mechanics School, also at Randolph. His first tour of duty ended on 26 June 1937 for that is where the paper trail begins. On that date he was discharged, at the convenience of the government (a standard military practice) to re-enlist. At the time his Rank was Private with a 6th Class Technical Specialist rating. That meant that he had completed the 1st step in a 6 step process as an Aircraft Mechanic. He re-enlisted the following day., His record shows that on 15 June 1938, he passed the test for Aircraft mechanic (Carburetor Specialist) with a grade of 86%.

An interesting note is the insignia of rank of the day, long forgotten by most but the most intense historians. In 1920, Congress authorized Specialist pay for the first 2 pay grades Private and Private First Class. Specialist ratings ran from 1st Class for the most experienced to 6th Class, which was the entry level. Though not officially authorized by the Army, many Specialists wore stripes to indicate their level of specialty with one stripe for 6th Class and added one more stripe for each level attained up to six. Thus, Patton as a Private First Class/Specialist 1st Class, could wear 6 inverted stripes under his single PFC chevron. Joe Pesec, a friend of Patton's in Hawaii based 5th Bomb Group, confirms that he wore the one-up/six-down cheverons.

ADMINISTRATION BUILDING
RANDOLPH FIELD TEXAS
PATTON'S FIRST DUTY STATION

Pattons Ground School Class 1936
SERVICE AT RANDOLPH FIELD, TEXAS

In December 1939, still stationed at Randolph, he was again discharged to re-enlist. At this time he had moved to 2nd Class Specialist. On 8 December he re-enlisted and was immediately promoted to Sergeant. He skipped the grade of Corporal which was an indication of superior performance for promotions in the "old army" were normally very slow in coming and to skip a grade was exceptional. This is our very first official record that William Wyatt Patton Junior was indeed, an exceptional soldier!

SERVICE AT HICKAM FIELD, HAWAII

The two friends served together for 6 years at Randolph and Ross had the pleasure of seeing his young protégé grow from a young recruit to a seasoned non-commissioned officer and expert mechanic. They were soon to part but fate would bring them together again in service to their country.

Sergeant/Air mechanic 1st Class William W. Patton Jr. was issued Special Order Number 44 dated 26 March 1944, from Headquarters Randolph Field, Texas. He was instructed therein to report to Ft. McDowell, California not later than 30 April 1940 for the purpose of sailing from San Francisco, California to Hawaii on 1 May 1940. He was transferred in an unassigned status and was posted to the 5th Bomb Group at Hickam, Airfield shortly after arrival. As evidenced by notations in his Enlisted Record he qualified as an Aerial Gunner on 25 October 1940 per Special Order #148 of the 5th Bomb Group at Hickam.

AUTHOR'S NOTE: There is a bit of a mystery associated with this qualification as family tradition states that he participated as an Aerial gunner on a B-17 at the Battle of Midway on 4-6 June 1942. However, Air Force records do not confirm him on any of the crew lists in that campaign. Doug Hicks, who was a close friend during Patton's Hawaii tours is adamant that Patton did serve at Midway and furthermore, shot down 2 Japanese airplanes. Ross Langley and Joe Pesec also confirm this claim.

On 12 September 1940 he was promoted from Sergeant to Staff Sergeant and he attained the rank of Technical Sergeant on 1 February 1942 and then to Master Sergeant on 1 September 1942. The quality of Patton's Performance is dramatically illustrated by his very rapid promotions through the ranks.

> NOTE: In 1942 the Army Air Corps was re-designated The Army Air Force

At this point we run into our first little mysteries It comes in a letter dated 7 April 1940 and is a commendation for William Wyatt Patton Junior by Major B.E. Allen, Commander of the 42nd Bomb Squadron. It commends the outstanding performance of Staff Sergeant Patton and states that Patton had been under Major Allen's command most of that time. The mystery comes in the fact, according to the Department of the Air Force publication, COMBAT SQUADRONS OF THE AIR FORCE IN WORLD WAR II, the 42nd Bomb Squadron was always a part of the 11th Bomb group and Patton was, according to his records, always in the 31st Squadron of the 5th Group. in the fact the letter addressed Patton as Staff Sergeant when in fact he was not promoted until September 1940.

DECEMBER 7TH 1941 AT PEARL HARBOR
AND HICKHAM FIELD, HAWAII

Finding members of the 5th Bomb Group and other members of the Army who served with William Patton not only gave us information about him but also provided eye witness views of the Japanese attack on that fateful Sunday morning

Doug Hicks - Arlington Texas

Finding Doug was clear evidence that I was ordained to tell Patton's story. It all transpired through a marvelous organization called the 8th Air Force Historical Society and the great editor of their fine newsletter, Doctor Walter Brown.

I asked Doc Brown to please publish an article which sought military comrades and information on Patton. The results were incredibly rewarding. They brought me in contact with John Lansing and John Hinner of the Aphrodite project and Doug Hicks, who served with Patton in Hawaii, thru flight training and in the 94th Bomb Group. What a find! But that was only a part of the gift......***Doug lives just 8 blocks from my home!!!!!*** As soon as we had completed our initial telephone conversation and the fact that he was a neighbor was revealed, I was at his home in 4 minutes flat where we spent 3 wonderful hours in conversation and photography.

Doug Hicks military history is a great story, typical of the highs and lows we all faced, with the marvelous addition of his 4 year friendship with William Patton. It begins with his entry into this world in 1918 in Greenville, Texas and Schooling in Amarillo, Texas. His interest in military aviation and the gathering war clouds prompted his enlistment in the Air Corps on 6 June 1941 at Barksdale Army Air Base in Bossier City, Louisiana, with his goal to enter the aviation cadet program as a pilot trainee. After 3 months basic training Off in La Hoya, California, his expectations of assignment to pilot training were rudely interrupted by orders to proceed to San Francisco for shipment to Hawaii. The August 1941 trip over was another horror story with thousands of troops, stuffed in the bowels of a steaming hot ship, with Dysentery and Seasickness flooring 99% of the troops.*(I can relate to that as I went exactly the same type of experience).* Fortunately, Doug was among the 1 % that was not disabled by illness. *(Equally fortunate, I also escaped illness on my trip).*

Arriving in Hawaii, Doug says there were so many new troops being shipped in that there were no quarters to house them. They were moved constantly, sometimes to barracks but mostly in tents and including World War I type dugouts With log roofs that they constructed themselves. This gypsy existence lasted thru his full tour of August 1941 through December 1942 with Schofield Barracks as a final and best destination.

<u>December 7th 1941</u> proved to be a most interesting day for Doug. Bivouacked at the then barren southwest corner of Oahu, on the west side of the channel opposite Hickam Field, Doug and his mates had a ringside seat for the deadly festivities that were to transpire that fateful morning. They had been transferred to the site for small arms practice and were sleeping in pup tents when the action began. At approximately 7:55 AM, they were awakened by the sound of many aircraft and massive explosions. At first they thought it was Navy maneuvers but quickly realized that this was war! Dressing quickly and grabbing their weapons, (Doug had a Browning automatic rifle) they watched in awe as 3 groups of Japanese bombers and torpedo planes, coming from a northwesterly direction, passed over them to the north and south. as the aircraft headed for EWA Navy Airfield, Hickam Field and Battleship Row in Pearl Harbor,

The ammo boxes were locked because all officers were in town and had the keys! The non-commissioned officers soon took action and broke the boxes open and issued ammo to all of the troops who began blazing away. Doug repeatedly emptied his BAR and, although not able to provide proof positive, believe that his group did their part in scoring lots of hits and perhaps downing an enemy aircraft or two. He noted that periodically, his group was noted by the attacking pilots and would drop the nose of their aircraft and fire a burst at the troops. Just when they thought the attack was easing, another group of Japanese bombers came in from the northeast. Another round of gunfire followed. No injuries were noted from this fire. As all over the island, friendly fire was the greatest danger. That afternoon, Hicks and his comrades were trucked north, to a fort whose name he could not remember, where they were set to the task of building dugouts. He recalls much hard labor digging small room sized holes in lava rock, covering the holes with logs and then covering the logs with rocks and soil.

Doug Hicks <u>finally had his opportunity, in the winter of 1942</u>, to enter the cadet program preliminaries when he was authorized to began written, psychological and physiological exams necessary to qualify for the program. There he met Patton and they became best friends. Through, Primary, Basic and Advanced flight training, B-17 transition school and combat crew training they were together. The match continued with assignment to the 331st Squadron of the 94th Bomb Group and the trip overseas. There, the intensity of training and the grueling combat missions left them little time to be together and eventually they lost contact when Patton went to the 388th Bomb Group Aphrodite mission at Fersfield. *Doug did not know of Pattons fate until I contacted him with the news in 2004.*

Several of Patton's 5BG mates were located as well as others who were in the group and in the 31st Squadron but did not know Patton. Here are some reminisces from these veterans

Doug Allen - "My memories of Pat only includes the short time, though it seemed long, when the Japanese dive bombers had dropped their bombs and came in low and strafed with forward guns firing and the rear gunner using his. They (the rear gunner) seemed to stand up while shooting to disable our bomber, B-17D (marked 5B-1) which had no power turrets. I guess they didn't bother trying to kill the few of us. John (Jackie) Hoagland and I took a tug and a little trailer with a waist gun, 50 caliber, and belts of ammo from the armament shack in the hangar and took it across the field to the above mentioned planes. They were parked across the field where they had been building a bunker to protect the airplanes. We tried to set up the gun and get it ready to fight back but the Jap planes started strafing other planes near us and we jumped out just in time. Hoagland, who was a small guy, hunkered down behind a wheel and I took one or two steps and fell on my face. When I opened my eyes it was like in the movies with bullets kicking up the dust within inches. Our planes engines and cockpit were burning both tires were flat. Hoagland wasn't settled before the 2nd Jap plane started to strafe so we got behind a pile of cement bricks that were piled up for the builders and there was Patton and a couple of guys whom I cannot remember. The only other guy in sight was me with my .45 pistol. I managed to shoot a couple of clips at the attacking planes and afterwards I remember Patton laughing about my strange language as I was shooting. I can't remember the rest of that day whether we had anything to eat or drink. We slept without mosquito netting and were badly chewed up.

Around midnite on the 7th, we heard firing and that lit up the sky over Pearl Harbor way. Planes had been in from our carriers and the sad story is that some were shot down by friendly fire. I don't remember seeing Patton again. I had known him casually as a mechanic on our B-17. I was in the armament section. Someone, I think it was Charles Werntz, told me that 5B-1 was fixed up and was the plane that Eddie Rickenbacker and crew went down in the Pacific and they were at sea in rubber life rafts for many days. He was on some kind of assignment for the War Department and headed for Australia. Remember that.

The Patton mystery for me, started when I was reading the Fresno newspaper in February 2001 and saw an article about discovering his remains in an airplane in France. A very sad reminder."

Elman Lemley- "Thank you for your letter. When I opened it and saw Patton's picture I became very excited. I knew him immediately and As I read, I was saddened to learn of his fate. I can certainly speak well of him as we were good friends for over 2 years. From 1939 to 1942 I was in Headquarters & Headquarters Squadron of the 5th Bomb Group at Hickham Field in Hawaii. I don't remember seeing him very much after the raid as we were shuffled around so much.

As I recall, when the first attack struck, I was on my bunk reading the Sunday paper. The first explosion I thought was definitely at Pearl Harbor. Moments later there were many explosions. The Arizona, Oklahoma and West Virginia were receiving torpedoes.

Then our barracks and hangars received bombs and strafing. The barracks wing next to mine took a direct bomb hit. I was on the third floor and could see the Rising Sun insignia coming around the corner on the Jap fighter. I could look right out at the pilot. I threw on my coveralls and ran downstairs to the first floor. Where I was forced under a stairway of concrete and steel by other troops. Now I was thinking of my plane on the ramp, a B-17D and I was the Crew Chief. One of my mechanics, Bill Simons, and I decided to go for it. Going outside, we saw hangars and planes in flames and flooding from blown water mains plus the sad sight of the injured and dead. Simons and I got to our plane and saw it had not been damaged very much although surrounded with burning planes and the hangar.

We jumped in the plane and hit all four starters and taxied out on the field toward our bunker. While underway the Japs saw our movement and three fighters made a firing pass at us. We saw them circling for another pass so we cut the switches and bailed out with the plane still rolling. Others had jumped into our plane just to get away from the flight line. One had been hit and was badly wounded. Leaving the plane we ran toward a test block building when the strafers came by again. Simons got hit in the leg but I was lucky...I thought. In a few minutes the Japs left and, not knowing why, we went back to the hangar area. Shortly after we saw waves of Japs coming overhead and could see them dropping bombs. We ran into the engineering office attached to the hangar just as bombs began to explode. The hangar got a direct hit. At that moment the ceiling and walls were crumbling and swaying. We ran outside and stood along the hangar wall and the strafing began again. I have a souvenir .....a bullet which hit 6 inches above my head.

I was so lucky as I moved the only B-17 from the ramps during both attacks. Oh yes, I don't know where I got it but I am still carrying a little piece of shrapnel in my butt!

Charles Werntz –<u>Charles knew Patton very well</u> and was kind enough to pass along some photos of the Hickham days and to tell me a story or two. First off he made it clear that "Pat", as most knew him, was an extremely nice person whom everybody liked but was quick add that he was still miffed about an incident related to the December 7th experience. "I had a camera but Pat did not so I was the one always taking pictures for him to send home. On the day of infamy I had the presence of mind to snap a number of pictures of the carnage and one was of a big clock inside our bombed out hangar which had stopped at the exact moment that the first bomb had hit. Pat left Hawaii before I did so I gave him the negatives to take home for safekeeping. I never saw them again. When I finally came back to the US after the war I tried to find the Patton family but was unsuccessful.

Dick Modling- "<u>Your letter got me in gear</u> to check some memorabilia in my file cabinet and within that mess was a December 1940, Headquarters Squadron photo showing Patton to be a Staff Sergeant in my outfit. At that time it was lofty rank and I was a 2–striper, top row, second from the left. We tended to buddy-up according to rank. I was a Flight Engineer on a B-18 at Hickam. It was really a DC-3 outfitted with manual turrets and a puny bomb rack that occasionally function properly and I considered this airplane the most ineffective, pieced together, patched up flying machine ever to hit the skies. Later we got B-17's.

As for the 7 December attack, I recall that the enlisted mess hall at the center of the barracks wing, had a mural depicting Pelee the Hawaiian Godess of Fire legend. Pele suffered serious damage to her right breast during the attack but for some time was left intact. Perhaps to remind all of us that we had desperate enemies and gave us reason to go after the bastard hammer and tong!

To the family of Patton I say: he was a genuine hero...he is my everlasting brother....

Joe Pesec- "Patton and I were in the headquarters Squadron together and I remember that everybody liked him. He a really nice guy. He was a B-17 Crew Chief flew combat missions during the battle of Midway. Patton also played the Catchers position on the squadron baseball team."

Other Pearl Harbor Veterans

Others of the 5BG were contacted but did not remember knowing Patton. However, these gentlemen were a delight to converse with and had many exciting tales of the 7 December 1941 attack by the Japs.

David Miller- David has passed on but I was able to contact his son-in-law **Bill Stewart** who did provide me with t wonderful set of photographs of 5th Bomb Group personnel at Hickam Field in the 1940's.

Joe Sybulski- Through clerical error, Joe is listed in the 5th Bomb group but was actually in the 11BG, across the taxiway from the 5th. He states that "during the attack I ran to the control tower because I remembered a flight of B-17's coming in from the west coast.

PILOT TRAINING

Doug Hicks finally got his release from the Coast Artillery and became Air Corps in the Fall of 1942. He immediately applied for Aviation Cadet training, which had always been his goal. During the Cadet exams he met Patton and the 2 became fast friends, remaining together through pilot training, B-17 transition and early assignment with the 94th Bomb Group in England.

Preflight School

Upon successfully completion of their Aviation Cadet exams, Patton and Hicks reported to Santa Ana Air Base in Santa Ana, California to begin Preflight Training. Here they met Jim Shawhan an Arthur Ford to make up the quartet that were to be close friends thru flight training and flying Bombers in the 8th Air Force in Europe. Here too, Patton was reunited with his cousin from home, Ross Langley, who was stationed in Santa Ana at Headquarters of the Western Training Command. Patton's and Hick's orders stated that they were to report on News Years Day 1943 to be enrolled in Class 43-J and that their courses extended to 16 April 1943. Preflight Training was designed to prepare the Cadet with skills that he would need in addition that required to operate an aircraft. It was normally a 10 week course that included 30 hours of aircraft and ship recognition; 48 hours of Morse Code; 24 hours of Physics; 20 hours of Mathematics; 18 hours of map and chart study with daily physical and military training. As the 2 lads spent some 15 weeks at Santa Ana, it is assumed that there was a waiting period prior to entering Preflight and some additional waiting before being assigned to Primary.

Primary Flight School

On 16 April Patton and Hicks reported to the Ontario, California airport which was operated by the Cal-Aero Academy, a civilian organization, under contract to the Army Air Corps and administered by the 2nd Air Force Flight Training Detachment. The school was divided into 6 squadrons with an Army Officer as a Supervisor and 3 or 4 Flight Instructors in each Squadron. While it is normal to allow some travel time between bases, Patton's record indicates that he reported to Primary Flight Training the same day that Preflight was completed. Since Ontario is less than 50 miles from Santa Ana, that is a practical consideration. Primary Flight Training introduced the fledgling aviator to the airplane for the very first time and instructed him in the fundamentals of aircraft operation.

The vehicle of choice for this phase of training was the rugged Stearman PT-13A open cockpit biplane. It was a wood, steel and aluminum structured, fabric covered, 225 horsepower little workhorse, beloved by all who flew it, including yours truly. The instructor sat in the forward cockpit and the student in the rear. Communications was one way, instructor to student! The course consisted of, as the name implies. instruction of the primary flying lessons: how to start, takeoff and land the airplane. Then when the instructor feels the student is ready, the first student solo flight; the greatest thrill a pilot ever experiences! It can be safely assumed that Patton soloed in minimum time. Primary also included 94 hours of ground school and 54 hours of military training.

Slipstream

In the early morning California sunlight,
Stearman PT-13A "Kadyet"
Primary trainers are prepared for the days operations.

A VIEW FROM THE COMMANDERS OFFICE

Squadron Five - Class 43J . . .

Some of those big hulking squadrons called us "Gremlins"—our flight commander called us "his boys"—and our ground school instructors don't know what to call us.

SQUADRON 5 OF CLASS 43-J

Patton was assigned to Squadron 5 with Jim Shawhan while Doug Hicks and Arthur Ford were in Flight 7. Patton completed Primary flight training with a final flight of 17 minutes on 12 June 1943. His form 5 shows that he logged some 65.8 hours of flying time in this phase of training. With their instruction completed at Ontario, the lads awaited their orders for Basic Flight School. They began their processing out on 21 June departed for their new station on the following day.

PATTON WITH FLYING MATES- HE IS FAR LEFT

Squadron 5's instructor is seated at the center of the picture flanked by his 4 Primary Flight School students. William Patton is at the far left. Identity of the other students is unknown.

Basic Flight School

On 23 June 1943, the intrepid airmen, flush with their successful completion of phase one of their flying career, reported to Gardner Field, California to begin their Basic Flight training. While still in Southern California, the base was some ways from Ontario in the small town of Taft. The nearest large city is Bakersfield. The School and base was commanded by Colonel Herbert W. Anderson, a World War I pilot and veteran of the early fighting in the Pacific.

The Basic course consisted of 70 to 80 hours of flight time in the Vultee BT-13 nicknamed the "Vibrator." It was a 2 place, enclosed cockpit, trainer with a 450 horsepower engine. The BT-13 was a significant step up from the PT-13. With its increased horsepower, performance and weight, it handled differently and was less forgiving than the little "bamboo bomber" they had learned to fly in. There were a lot more instruments and controls which introduced these fledgling airmen to a world of procedures and checklists which would become a major part of their flying routine as their flying machines became more complex. They were to learn that good procedures are necessary to staying alive in a flying career. Basic course also included about 100 hours of Ground School which consisted of weather, navigation, aircraft mechanics and other courses. About 50 hours of Military Training was taken.

**VULTEE BT-13 BASIC TRAINER
NICKNAMED THE "VIBRATOR"**

There is a very significant process which takes place in the basic phase, one which effects each individual throughout his flying career. Each, on the basis of his performance, personality and to some degree, stature, is selected for a career path in different types of aircraft: Single Engine or Multi Engine. Cadets with more carefree, flamboyant

BASIC FLIGHT SCHOOL CADETS PATTON, FORD AND HICKS LOOKING MIGHTY HAPPY NEAR GRADUATION

and daring personalities and actions tended to be recommended for Single Engine Advanced Flight School where they usually ended up in Fighter Aircraft. The caveat in this situation was a limitation on height in deference to the smaller Fighter cockpits. Those with more serious personalities who did well in group situations and tended to think strategically, were recommended for Multi-Engine Advanced Flight School and ultimately flew Bomber or Transport aircraft. There were other factors that could impact the final decision with the primary consideration being the need at the time the selections were made.

Patton and Shawhan were assigned to Squadron 13 while Hicks and Ford was posted to 11 Squadron. Patton's Instructor was Lt. Stendahl. Patton logged a total of 80 flight hours which included 14 hours of instrument training. In addition, he had 11 hours of instrument time in the Link Trainer. The Link was the earliest form of Flight Simulator used by the Army Air Force and provided a safe and economical way to supplement in-flight instrument training in a true blind flying environment. With flying and ground courses completed on 25 August 1943, the processing out routine began once again for the "4 Musketeers." They were selected for Multi Engine Flight School and departed Gardner Field on 30 August. Again, the group remained in California and only had to travel north about 230 miles to their new base. Their destination was Stockton Field in Stockton, California where they reported in on 31 August 1943.

Multi Engine Advanced Flight School

On the last day of August 1943, the quartet arrived at their new base in Stockton to begin the final phase of their Aviation Cadet training. The Multi engine course length was scheduled for 10 weeks and consisted of 70 to 80 hours of flight in AT-17 and UC-78 airplanes, 60 hours of Ground School and 20 hours of Military training. The UC-78 "Bobcat" was a military version of the Cessna 5 place T-50 commercial transport, a fabric covered structure powered by two Jacobs 295 horsepower engines. The AT-17 had an identical airframe with slightly less powerful engines and minor changes in equipment. Both types were used interchangeably. It was affection ally known as the "Bamboo Bomber."

THE CESSNA AT-17 USED IN MULTI-ENGINE TRAINING

2ND LT WILLIAM W. PATTON JR.
ARMY AIR FORCE PILOT

The pride of accomplishment is clearly evident in this photo of Lt. Patton upon graduation from AAF Pilot School of Stockton Army Air Field, California

The flying training began on 5 September 1943 and proceeded though 29 October 1943. Patton logged a total of 75 hours and 55 minutes which included 14 hour and 30 minutes of instrument training. He also acquired some 10 hours and 20 minutes of Link time during this period. On 2 November 1943 Cadet days were ended with a discharge from the Cadet program. On 3 November, the joyous moment arrived when the 4 Amigos, Patton, Ford, Hicks and Shawhan pinned on their silver wings as pilots and their gold bars as Second Lieutenants in the US Army Air Force. What a celebration must have followed graduation. 163 other new 2nd lieutenants joined our little group in a farewell to their cadet days but not their student time. There was a lot more training to come! Farewells were said at Stockton and the 167 souls who began their Cadet training together in Santa Anna 11 months before, were off to their Transition Training assignments around the country. The Quartet were destined to split up here with Shawhan and Ford taking a different route from Patton and Hicks.

B-17 Transition Training

Departing Stockton on 3 November 1943, Patton and Hicks reported to the 38th Flight Training Wing at Hobbs Air Base in Hobbs, New Mexico on 4 November 1943.

CLASS 43-J B-17 TRANSITION TRAINING CLASS

Hobbs Army Air Field, New Mexico

Patton and Hicks were still together and were introduced to the famous B-17 "Flying Fortress" bomber which was the backbone of the bomber fleet in the European phase of WW II combat. The training began immediately upon arrival and included Ground School, Marksmanship,

Link Trainer, Bomb Trainer, Physical Training and Operational Flight Training. **Ground School** - Courses consisted of 162 hours of class room instruction in Engineering, 30 hours of Navigation, 15 hours of Radio, 10 hours of Meteorology(weather), 3 hours First Aid, 8 hours Oxygen, 6 hours of Radio Code, 3 hours of Bombing Theory, 44 hours of Maintenance Engineering, and 6 hours covering the responsibilities and duties of an Airplane Commander. This totaled 162 hours.

Link Trainer - Patton logged some 16 hours of Link Trainer time. The Link Trainer was a very early day, ground based Flight Simulator which allowed pilots to simulate flying of the aircraft while using only instruments to operate and navigate the aircraft. This was accomplished "under the hood" which is the term used for training in a blacked out cockpit with only the instruments to provide direction, height, velocity and direction of the airplane.

Bomb Trainer – In 4 hours of training he actually learned the duties of the Bombardier using the Norden Bomb Sight. This was another simulator, which consisted of a tubular steel platform, with seat for an occupant, and the bomb sight. On the floor was a scaled map of a target area. It did teach the fundamentals of bomb dropping. This too, was an important bit of training as it helped the pilots to understand the difficulties of accurate bombing and as a  subtle reminder the primary duty of the entire Crew was to bring the Bombardier and his weapons load to the target.

Weapons Qualification – Because each officer on a flight crew was armed with a 45 caliber automatic pistol, it was necessary for each to learn weapon safety, maintenance and marksmanship. As was typical of anyone firing only 40 rounds from this close quarters weapon, no medals were earned although he did fire a respectable 75%.

NOTE: Use of the 45 automatic, when facing the enemy on the ground was sometimes more dangerous to the user than to the enemy who would be most likely be equipped with a rifle. This made the pistol useless. A case that illustrates another danger of a side arm is that of **William Cullerton, P-51 Mustang Ace of the 355th Fighter Group of the 8th Air Force,** flying out of Steeple Morden, England. Bill was shot down in France and captured by German SS troops. Upon surrendering his pistol to the SS officer in charge, the officer proceeded to place the gun in Bill's stomach and shot him! Bill was left for

CAPT. BILL CULLERTON - 355TH FIGHTER GROUP

dead but survived and was taken to a French hospital where his life was treated by a German doctor who not only saved Cullerton's life but hid him from another German patrol and helped him escape! A dramatic example of the firearm and human behavior at opposite ends of the spectrum!

Physical Training – <u>This was a very important,</u> but not necessarily admired, phase of the program which included a variety of exercises plus cross country runs. Aircrew ultimately came to appreciate this toughening-up process when they encountered the physical and mental stresses of long combat missions over the Antiaircraft and Fighter filled skies of Europe.

Operational Flight Training – <u>Here, the newly graduated multi-engine pilot</u> receives his introduction to the combat machinery he was destined to fly in combat. In this case, the B-17F Flying Fortress. The

F- models were the most available version for training purposes as they were being phased out of combat in favor of the more heavily armed G-model. The flight characteristics of the F were similar enough to the G to assure that transition to the more modern version they were to fly in combat was not difficult.

Learning to operate the specific aircraft was not the only goal of the transition program. The training also consisted of teaching familiarity with the environment in which they would soon experience when they reached an operational such as flying in formation with several other

B-17's, simulated and actual instrument flying, both of which he would see plenty of when he reached his assigned bomber unit, plus night operations and both pilot and co-pilot duties.

Patton begin his B-17 flight training on 19 November 1943 and flew a total of 11 hours and 5 minutes in 3 days of operations, all in the left hand seat as a Student Pilot.

The month of December produced the most intense period of his B-17 training with a total of 52 hours in the cockpit over a period of 14 days. During these flights he accumulated the majority of hours as Student Pilot with some Co-pilot and First Pilot hours. Included were significant night and instrument hours. Since no flying took place between the 22nd and 29th, it is assumed that the class stood down for the Christmas holidays.

January, while not as heavy as December, was still a month with plenty of flying in addition to all of the other training activities. In frosty winter weather Lt. Patton was able to put in 42 hours in the B-17 cockpit. Here again, the time was fairly evenly distributed between co-pilot, dual instruction, first pilot day/night, instrument and night duties. Pattons final training flight at Hobbs Field took place on 15 January 1943. His Certificates for flying and ground school Are dated 19 January 1944.

Sioux City Army Air Base, Iowa – <u>Pattons Form 5 shows no additional entries</u> until March 1944. It assumed that the period between 19 January and 1 March were consumed by transfer to the new and some well earned leave. SCAAB was home of the 393rd Combat Crew Training to which Patton and Hicks were now assigned. Here they were to continue to team. Added to the crew were 9 other personnel necessary to successfully prosecute combat missions. Included in the complement were the Co-pilot, Navigator, Bombardier, Radio Operator, Flight Engineer/Top Turret Gunner, Right & Left Waist Gunners, Ball Turret Gunner and Tail Gunner. They were identified as Crew 3352.

B-17F FLYING FORTRESS

Through the Primary and Basic phases of training, the students learned their lessons as individuals in a single cockpit. In Advanced and Transition training they enjoyed the company of an instructor or co-pilot in the other seat but now, Combat Crew Training placed them in the position of being head of a small "family." While each man in the crew had individual responsibilities, the pilot is the airplane commander, accountable for every person and every action on every flight of the bomber. This is an awesome responsibility when the ultimate task is the daily life and death struggle of combat. Patton was not only a dedicated and responsible airman, he was also older and more experienced than most of his contemporaries. The crew was always in good hands with Lt. William Wyatt Patton.

Training at Sioux City began on 1 March 1944 with a fairly light flying schedule and considerable ground training during the first 2 weeks. The second half of the month, however, was intense with 14 straight days of flying. Some 35 plus hours were logged. During this period Patton was introduced to the B-17G, which would be the machine he was to fly in combat. About 21 hours was flown in the G-model.

The month of April began with a flight of one hour and 30 minute night flight as First pilot. This was to be a very heavy schedule with a total of 71 hours and 40 minutes in 22 flights. This is a lot of flying hours and all in the left seat as first pilot. Getting acquainted with the entire crew, establishing crew discipline and developing confidence in his role as the leader of this team was as important as the technical aspects of the training.

On the 15th of April Patton received a certificate of proficiency as a B-17F & B-17G Aircraft Commander, signed by Capt. James K. David. On 26 April he received his White Card instrument certificate after a proficiency flight examination conducted by 1st Lt. James S. Law.

The month of May was very light operationally, with only 6:25 logged on the 1st through the 8th. On the 16th of May Patton departed Sioux City AM for the air base at Kerney, Nebraska where he was assigned his own B-17G and prepared to depart for Europe.

CHAPTER 6

INTO COMBAT

Patton had a fine crew that had trained together for months. He was presented with a brand new B-17 and it was time to go to war. He was a happy soldier, newly promoted, ready and anxious to do his part After a very successful start to his combat career, problems, not of his making were to dog him constantly. Fate would not be kind to this fine young man

ON HIS WAY

Just before departing for England, Patton received a pleasant surprise when he was promoted to the rank of First Lieutenant confirmed by War Department Special Order 116, dated 15 May 1944. With shiny new B-17 in hand and and eager crew on board, Patton departed for England on 20 May 1944. Pattons letter to his Mother, postmarked 19 May, 1944, written the day before he departed for England, states. This letter is the last piece of correspondence in the Patton files.

Voyage To England

It was to be a voyage with several stops and plenty of excitement. In an intereview with **Doug Hicks** his close friend from enlisted days in Hawaii, Flight Training and the 94th Bomb group, I learned that he, Patton and a number of other crews departed Kerney, Nebraska on

20 May 1944, bound for Grenier Field, New Hampshire. There they assembled with a large group of B-17's scheduled to make a mass flight to England via Goose Bay Laborador. The assembled B-17's totaled 66 in all. Doug Hicks described the flight as a near disaster in the midst of a major storm. Practically everyone had difficulties and wound up scattered all over the northern US and southern Canada. Only a handful of the group arrived on schedule. The flight to England featured better weather but met with equal confusion because the Germans were jamming radio signals and generating false navigational beams. Patton logged 26 hours and 25 minutes on this journey, of which 10 hours was on instruments.

In Earls Colne England with the 94th Bomb Group

Patton and his crew reported to the 94th Bomb Group at station 358 in Earls Colne, England on 23 May 1944. The 94th was a part of the 4th Combat Wing of the 8th Air Force. The 94th was commanded by Colonel Charles B. Dougher who had taken over the group when Brigadier General Fred Castle moved up to command the 4th Combat Wing in April 1944. Castle was killed in action on Christmas eve 1944 and was awarded the Congressional Medal of Honor for heroism in that combat action. The stay at Earls Colne was to be a short one for on 15 June 1944, the entire 94th Group moved a few miles north to station 489 at Bury St. Edmunds.

William W Patton and unidentified
crewman, thought to be a co-pilot

Into combat with the 94th bomb group

Patton was assigned to the 331st Bomb Squadron and began his initial combat. training on 20 May. According to **Doug Hicks**, though they were in the same Squadron, training was so intensive, followed by indoctrination into combat, that little time was left for anything else. Consequently, Hicks and Patton saw little of each during the month of June 1944. As a result, Doug could add little to the story for this period of Patton's service. Patton and his crew logged some 26 hours and 25 minutes through 23 May. From then until mid June there was no more flying due to the transfer of the 94th Bomb group to Bury St Edmund. On 12 and 13 June, he logged 3:15 in 2 training.

331st Bomb Squadron crew listing

With the help of English buddy, **Tony Plowright,** the 331st Bomb Squadron Pilot List and the Patton Crew Load List were located. The Crew Load List for June 1944 consisted of:

Pilot-.W.W. Patton, Co-Pilot-R.L. Stiles, Navigator-A.L. Hall, Bombardier-K.J. Nefzger

Top turret Gunner-F. Conger, Ball turret Gunner-J.M. Binda, Tail Gunner-R.A. Mickley

Right Waist Gunner-R.J. Poll, Left Waist Gunner-D. Gilbert, Radio Operator-B.F. Younginer

Others who flew missions on the Patton crew as replacements included: Tail Turret-W.E. Lewis, Tail Turret-E.C. Wright, Waist Gunner-W.L. Siebold, Radio Operator-E.B. Cassler And Waist Gunner-A.E. Soltman

331ST BOMB SQUADRON COMBAT OPERATIONS

The mission information presented here is drawn from The 331st Bomb Squadron official "War Diary" log for June 1944, Roger Freeman "War

Diary" book. and Lt. Patton's Form 5 Individual Flight Record. The 331st Bomb Squadron War Diary is a log of Squadron flight operations, maintained by the Intelligence Section, in which entries were made each day. A single paragraph summarizes the action of the day. The June 1944 War diary was prepared by ᵗ Lt. Sherman, 331BS Intelligence Officer.

For those not familiar with the form 5, it is the official record of flight time. Officially designated as INDIVIDUAL FLIGHT RECORD - War Department AAF Form 5 –Approved Dec 7, 1942. It is one of the most important documents in an Airman's file because of its impact in so many areas of a Flying Officers career. It is a record of all o f his flying time, posted daily on a flight by flight basis, issued monthly and certified correct by the Operations Officer of the assigned unit. It is a key document for the historian and Patton's Form 5's were a major source of information in tracking his history.

June 1944 Missions

Combat operations for Patton and his crew began on 14 June 1944. Their combat missions are summarized as follows:

Mission # 1 on 14 June - Bombed 12 different targets in Northern France -This raid involved 1525 bombers from the 3 Air Divisions with the primary targets being Airfields, Supply Depots and Contruction Sites. The 3AD launched 351 B-17's and 191 B-24's in 4 groups. The 94th was at full squadron strength with no losses over the target but one B-17 crashed on landing at Bury St. Edmunds. *Florannes A/D was the 331BS target for the day. Bombed with good result. Flak was meager and inaccurate. No E/A were encountered. Pilots participating included Allison, Davis, Dean, Gette, Griffitt and Patton. Patton logged 5:45 flying as co-pilot on this his first combat mission.*

==

The 15th and 16th of June were training days. *Patton logged 2:20 co-pilot time and 1:40 as First **Pilot***

Mission #2 on 18 June - Bombed Hannover-Misburg and Breman, Germany

This was a 1378 plane mission with 3rd Division contributing 368 bombers from 4 Groups. Primary targets were Oil refineries and Luftwaffe Control Centers. Because of bad weather, Targets of Opportunity were also hit. All 94BG aircraft returned safely. *Once again PFF technique was used to bomb Misburg with results unknown. The target was well defended by intense and accurate flak. Approximately 20 E/A were observed but no attacks were made on the Group. Pilots participating were Allison, Dean, Gette. Griffitt, Jacobs, Jester, Manz, Moser, Peterson, Vogel and* **Patton.**

7:35 was logged by Patton as First Pilot.

----

20 June was another training day and 2:10 logged as First Pilot

----

Mission #3 on - 21 June Bombed Berlin, Basdorf and Rhuland

1234 airplanes were assigned to this mission with 390 from the 3rd Division. The city of Berlin and Basdorf were hit as well as Oil installations at Ruhland. The 94th lost one B-17. *Once again Berlin is hit by the 331BS. Bombing was a combination of visual and PFF with good results. Flak was intense and accurate at the target. 15 E/A were seen in the vicinity of the target. 331st Squadron aircraft piloted by Jester, Moser, Moriarity,* **Patton**, *Dean, Vogel, Griffitt, Allison, Gette, Davis and Jacobs participated in this raid.* Pattons crew included CP-Stiles, N-Hall, B-Nefzger, R-Younginer, TTG-Conger, BTG-Binda, TG-Mickley, RWG-Poll and LWG-Gilbert. *Flying time credited to Patton on this mission was 7:35.*

Mission # 4 on 22 June - Bombed 6 targets in Northern and Central France

MarshallingYards, Railroads, Airfields and V-Weapon sites at Melun, Nucourt, Brie-Comte-Robert Sug, Lieusant, and Entampes were hit by 216 B-17's of the 3rd Division. Total force for the mission was 1099 B-17's and B-24's. The 94th had no losses. *Nucourt Military Installation was the 331BS target for today. Hit with good results. The flak at the target was moderate and very accurate but no E/A were encountered.* Pilots taking part were Davis, Dean, Gette, **Hicks**, Jacobs, Jester, Manz, Moriarity, **Patton**, Petersank, and Whorton. All aircraft returned safely. W.E. Lewis substituted for J.E. Conger as Top turret Gunner for this mission. A total of 7:00 First Pilot time was logged by Patton

----

Mission #5 on 23 June - Bombed 5 targets in North Central France
The 3rd Division contributed 109 B-17's out of a total force of 568 bombers. The 8AF hit Missile Sites, Airfields and Marshalling Yards with the 3AD concentrating on Marshalling Yards at Nanteuil. All 94BG aircraft returned safely. Aircraft flown by Pilots Jester, Hicks, Moriarty, Davis, **Patton,** and Spenst participated in this mission. Substitutes on the Patton crew included **E.C. Wright** as Top Turret Gunner and **W.L. Siebold** as Left Waist Gunner. *Epernay was the scheduled 331 BS target for today but weather made bombing impossible so bombs were brought back. No aircraft missing. On this flight, Patton added 6:20 First Pilot time to his Combat Log.*

Mission # 6 on 25 June - bombed 11 targets in North and Central France
1121 bombers were put in the air this day with the 3rd Division contributing 189 B-17's for raids on Airfields at Paris-Orly & Etampes/ Mondesir; bridges at Auxerre, Soigny & Sens plus other targets at Clamecy, Nogent, Nanteuil, Folous and Romilly-Sur-Seine and also dropped supplies to French Partisans *Special mission to France was the order of the day for the 331BS. Aircraft piloted by Pilots Peterson, Jester, Gette, Schumaker, Allison, Pursglove, **Patton**, Griffit, Moser, **Hicks** and Dean were on this raid. All crews returned safely.* On Pattons crew, substitutions included E.C. Wright as Top Turret Gunner, W.L.Siebold as Right Waist Gunner and A.E. Soltman as as Left Waist gunner. *A total of 9:20 was logged by Patton as First Pilot.* **6-5**

Mission #7 on 26 June - Recalled shortly after mission launched
A total of 1:20 First Pilot was credited for this effort

Mission #8 on 29 June - Bombed Bohlen and Wittenberg, Germany
A total force of 1150 bombers hit multiple targets in Germany with the 3rd Division contributing 770 B-17's and B-24's. 179 of the 3AD B-17's hit Oil Industry structures in Bohlen and Wittenberg. The 94BG Suffered no losses. *Wittenberg was the 331BS target for today. Bombing results were very good. Flack from Bohlen was very accurate and intense. A number of E/A were observed but driven off by friendly escort. part were All crews returned safely. 331ST aircraft piloted by Moriarty,* **Patton,** *Peterson, Dean, Pursglove, Grifitt and Allison took part in this raid. Lt's Wendt, Manz and Purnell crews completed their tours this month.* Crew substitutions on the Patton airplane included Radio-E.B. Cassler, Top Turret-E.C. Wright, Right Waist-W.L. Siebold and Left Waist-A.E. Soltman. *First pilot time logged by Patton was 8:05 on this his final bombing mission.*

Other 94th Bomb Group pilots on June 1944 missions- In My 5 year search for other pilots of the 94th Bomb Group and 331st Bomb Squadron yielded **Doug Hicks and Bob Allison.** Hick's early relationship with Patton has been previously recorded while his further adventures are described below. I found Bob Allison with the assistance of a dear lady, **Debi Robinson**, President of the 94BG Association. Bob also sent me photos.

Doug Hicks-Doug flew on the same missions as Patton on 22, 23 and 25 June 1944. Hicks flew regularly until 6 August 1944 when his B-17 was badly damaged by flack on a mission to Berlin but managed to stagger back to the coast of Holland where he ditched in the North Sea, about 17 miles offshore. The airplane stayed afloat for enough time for the crew to escape the wreckage. 7 of the crew were on one side of the airplane in rubber rafts while Hicks was on the other side extracting his badly wounded tail gunner, Danny DePauley and LH Waist Gunner, who was uninjured but in a panic. Only 2 rafts were available so Hicks was in the freezing water in his life jacket, holding on to the 2 dinghies to prevent them from floating away. Unfortunately, the other 7 crew members were carried away by the current but were picked up by

German Air-Sea Rescue sometime later. DePauley died shortly after the airplane evacuation. Hicks held on to the 2 rafts and suffered for 38 hours in the water. He had almost given up hope of rescue when, at dawn, a German rescue boat appeared and the 3 were recovered.

Hicks and his Waist Gunner were taken to a Dutch jail where they remained until transferred to a German Interrogation Center in Frankfurt. Hicks tried to escape from the Jail, which he describes as immaculately clean, during a Royal Air Force bombing of a nearby German troop installation. Unfortunately, he became wedged in the window after partially removing the bars, and was caught by the returning guard as the bombing stopped. The Guard's swinging rifle butt assisted Hicks to dislodge himself from the window. Hicks stated that he was mercifully relieved of the company of his Gunner when the transfer to Frankfurt took place. He remembers that this 18 year old caused him more grief than any other human being he ever encountered.

The Interrogation Center tour was a long one with unrelenting questioning and periodic blows on the shins with a metal bar. The Good Guy-Bad Guy routine included cigarettes and schnapps between abuse and question sessions. He was then transferred to Stalug Luft III in the center compound. There he languished thru the winter of 1944 until he and a fellow prisoner named Bob (last name not remembered) escaped and wandered through the German countryside for several days until captured by a group of Hungarian SS troops. They were then returned to Stalag Luft III.

BOB ALLISON-1944

BOB AND HELEN ALLISON-2006

BOB ALLLISON CREW-1944

During all of this period he had a nagging pain in the right side which was thought to be appendicitis. He was eventually allowed to go to another prison camp, one with mostly Russian POW's, where surgery was possible because the camp had 4 French medical personnel. The only anesthetic was spinal block medication so, after 3 shots, he was able to observe the operation up close and personal. He states that the French Medic held up the Appendix and said, "this is not chic." Hicks agreed that it was truly ugly. The Medic informed him that the organ was not diseased and shortly produced a long, skinny piece of shrapnel that had been the cause of the pain all along. Again, back to Stalag Luft III where he suffered his recovery over a period of several miserable weeks. Near the end of the war, he had another opportunity to escape and, this time, made his way to a unit of Pattons 3rd Army. Not long after that he was on his way home.

Bob Allison – Bob reportedly flew combat missions in the same formation with Patton on 14, 18, 21, 25 and 29 June 1944. This according to the 94BG Crew Load Lists. However, his personal files reflect only missions on the 14th, 18th and 21st of June 1944. Because the latter listed dates are drawn from Bob's Form 5, these are undoubtedly the correct dates. He went on to fly 26 missions and was seriously wounded in that final action. Bob enlisted in the Army Air Corps Aviation Cadet Program early in 1942 and graduated in 1943 as a member of class 43-I. He B-17 transition at Hobbs New Mexico and combat Crew Training at Alexandria.

July 1944 Activities by Patton - This is where a series of mysteries begin. There is no record of flying time for Patton during the month of July 1945. It is not a matter of a missing Form 5 for the June document ends with a total time of 629:35 and the August issue starts with 629:35. Patton departed the 94th Bomb Group after what is indicated as a good start to his combat tour. Because he was such an outstanding officer, the reason for not flying had to be something beyond his control. There is evidence that it was medically related. This based upon his August From 5 which ends with the statement: "Closed-Transferred to Hospital." In addition, the family recalls discussion about Patton having the Mumps while overseas. Mumps, though normally a mild childhood disease, can be quite difficult for an adult and especially an Airman.

About that time, Project Aphrodite was recruiting volunteers. We do know that he joined the 388th Bomb Group at Knettishall as evidenced by his Form 5 and a letter that he wrote in November 1944. The Aphrodite Project was an ill-fated experiment that featured radio controlled B-17's and B-24's which were dived into the target by an operator on the "Mother aircraft". The explosive laden B-17 had to take off at the hand of an experienced pilot, flown to a safe altitude, armed by an on-board engineer and then the pilot and engineer parachuted from the B-17, after control had been assumed by the Mother Ship.

We can imagine how Patton jumped at the chance to join the Aphrodite Project when volunteers were sought and told that they would only be away from their home unit for 3 weeks and would get credit for 5 missions. It seemed like the answer to prayer for this eager young airman who wanted only to get back into the air and do his part in the war. It seemed like the perfect opportunity to catch up on his missions in a very short period. But, like many military adventures, they don't work quite as advertised and volunteering does not produce the desired Results.

August 1944 Activities-Station 136-Fersfield Patton's Records for August 1944 reflect only 10 non-combat flights with the majority being 2 hours or less. On the 26th of August he made his final flight of the month and his form 5 is then marked "Transferred to Hospital." It also shows the assigned organization to be the 331st Squadron of the 94th Group and is signed by **Lt. Milton V. Eddy** as Assistant Operations Officer. However, <u>a Transmittal of Flying Time document</u> from

INDIVIDUAL FLIGHT RECORD

(1) SERIAL NO. O-752480   (2) NAME PATTON, WILLIAM W., JR. (3) RANK 1st Lt   (4) AGE 29

(5) PERS. CLASS 18   (6) BRANCH Army Air Forces   (7) STATION #136 APO 559

(8) ORGANIZATION ASSIGNED B   B   3rd B.Div   388th   560th
(9) ORGANIZATION ATTACHED

(10) PRESENT RATING & DATE P 11-3-43   (11) ORIGINAL RATING & DATE P 11-3-42
(12) TRANSFERRED FROM   (13) FLIGHT RESTRICTIONS None
(13) TRANSFERRED TO   (14) TRANSFER DATE

(17) MONTH Oct.

PERS CLASS		A.F.	COMMAND	WING	GROUP NO.	GROUP TYPE	SQUADRON NO.	SQUADRON TYPE	STATION	NO. YR.

	AIRCRAFT TYPE, MODEL & SERIES		FLYING	COMMAND PILOT	CO. PILOT	GROUND PILOT	FIRST PILOT DAY	FIRST PILOT NIGHT	RATED PERS. NON-PILOT	NON-RATED				SPECIAL INFORMATION			
1	B17D	1					2:00											
5	B17F	1					1:20											
24	B17D	1					2:00											
30	B17F	1					1:20											

CERTIFIED CORRECT

JOHN N. LITTLEJOHN JR.
1st Lt. Air Corps,
Operations Officer.

| COLUMN TOTALS | | 6:40 | |

	(42) TOTAL STUDENT PILOT TIME	(43) TOTAL FIRST PILOT TIME	(44) TOTAL PILOT TIME
(37) THIS MONTH		6:40	6:00
(38) PREVIOUS MONTHS THIS F.Y.		16:25	18:35
(39) THIS FISCAL YEAR		23:05	24:35
(40) PREVIOUS FISCAL YEARS		213:30 26:10	629:55
(41) TO DATE	275:55	236:35 26:10	654:30

	AIRCRAFT NO.	CARD NO. 1	CARD NO. 2	CARD NO. 3
	19 20	21 22 23 24 25 26	27 28 29 30 31	32 33 34 35

**AAF FORM 5 WITH PATTONS FINAL
FLIGHT TIME IN THE B-17**

Captain John M. Sande, Operations Officer of "Project Aphrodite" at Station 136, Fersfield, indicates that Pattons flying time for August 1944 was accomplished at Fersfield. Project Aphrodite was operated by a Detachment of the 388th Bomb Group at Fersfield. The 94th still maintaining Pattons Form 5 would indicate that he was attached to the 388th rather than being permanently assigned.

September 1944 Activities-Station 159-Wormingford

Patton's September 1944 Form 5 really confuses the issue. First of all it indicates Patton's organization to be The 560th Squadron of the 388th Bomb Group and the Station as 159 which is a Fighter Base at Wormingford, host base of the 55th Fighter Group and the 3rd Scouting Force. To top it off, there is a September <u>Transmittal of Flying Time</u> from the 388th Detachment at Fersfield to the 94th Bomb Group showing that his September flying was from Fersfield, home of Aphrodite.

To make this Form 5 even more amazing, it is signed by **O.V. Lancaster** as Assistant Operations Officer of the 3rd Scouting Force at Wormingford who is positively known to have been at Wormingford at the time. Wormingford is <u>not</u> noted by any historical publication, private or government, as a base for any 388th Bomb Group elements. Secondly, a conversation with **Dr. Vince Masters, 3rd Scouting Force Commander**, brought the response:*"there were no B-17's at Wormingford when I formed the 3rd Scouts." B-17's did not appear until February 1945 when the 3rd Weather and Scouting Force, made up of B-17's, was formed. By the 3rd Air Division."* To the contrary, and deepening the mystery, the fact remains that Patton's official flying records show that he spent the entire month at Wormingford, making 8 flights for a total of 16 hours and 25 minutes and was certified as such by O.V. Lancaster!

October 1944 Activities-Station 136-Fersfield

His Form 5 shows little activity with only 4 flights during the month for a total of 6 hours 40 minutes First Pilot time. This apparently included

3 training flights and one for real. **Roger Freeman's** records indicate that Patton made his one "hot" flight on 15 October 1944 flying B-17G 42-30066 with **Lt. J.W. Hinner** as co-pilot. After trimming the ship and arming the explosives, both safely bailed out near the English coastline and the "Mother Ship" took it to the target which was Heligoland Island, off the coast of Germany. The result was the same as previous missions, no targets were destroyed. Just another big bang and a huge hole in the ground. A telephone interview with John Hinner in late 2001 confirmed the mission but no detail was available. *Another documentary problem exposed is that Pattons Form 5 does <u>not</u> show a mission on 15 October 1944.* Only flights on the 1st, 3rd, 24th and 30th of October 1944 were recorded. with a total flight time as first pilot of 6 hours and 40 minutes in 3 separate flight includes 13 landings, apparently he was checking out another pilot.

November 1944-Station 136-Fersfield -The November Form 5 entries show another 7 hours and 55 minutes on flights of the 11th, 12th, 22nd, 25th and 29th. Curiously, the 11 November flight

Transfer requested - In late October or early November 1944, Patton must have decided that Aphrodite was a dead end for him and opted to leave through transfer to another organization. On 7 November he submitted a letter to the Commanding General of the 3rd Air Division, requesting transfer to a Photo Reconnaissance Group. Letter shown next page. His request was approved and on 17 December 1944 he received orders to report, not to a Photo recon Group but to the 55th Fighter Group at Wormingford.

This immediately immediately begs the question, why, after requesting assignment to a Photo Recon Group, was he transferred to a Fighter Group. If Patton was at Wormingford in September, it could possibly explain why he was ultimately assigned there after asking for transfer to a Photo Recon unit. His exposure to the newly formed 3rd Scouting Force, if that really happened, could have influenced him to seek assignment there. Another interesting aspect of this story is the fact that 3 other

Aphrodite pilots, besides Patton, were later assigned to the 3rd Scouting Force. They were **Noel E. Garvin(96BG), Russell Betts(96BG), and John Stein(390BG)**. Stein was shot down by another Mustang on 21 April 1945 and was MIA until 1948 when his remains were recovered from a Swedish lake. Betts has not been located as of this writing. These gentlemen may have had a hand in influencing Patton to come to the Scouts.

TRANSFER TO" CLOBBER COLLEGE"

The 55TH Fighter Group

Lt. Patton arrived at the 55th Fighter Group on 17 December 1944 and was assigned to the Fighter Transition Training Detachment of the 55th which was known as"Clobber College." All new pilots assigned to the 55th were required to attend ground and flight training to acquaint them with the P-51 Mustang and the Group operations procedures. **Lt. Herman J. Schoenenberg** was assigned as Patton's instructor. Ground School was probably conducted before Christmas and Flight Training immediately after Christmas. Patton's Form 5 shows a total of 2 flights. The first was his transition flight of 1 hour 30 minutes, with one take off and landing, on 28 December which earned him the 55th's Transition Flying Training Certificate of the same date. His certificate was signed by **Lt. Millard O. Anderson**, who went on to a distinguished career in the USAF after the war. Patton flew another 1 hour 20 minutes training flight on 31 December.

I found Mr. Schoenenberg in New York and questioned about, what seemed to me to be a rather short transition from the big and slow B-17 to the swift little Mustang. He indicated that it was not unusual for a short checkout when the student showed exceptional flying abilities. Apparently Patton fit that qualification which was certainly consistent with his outstanding performance in every aspect of his military career.

LT HERMAN SCHOENBERG-
55TH FIGHTER GROUP
PATTON'S P-51 FLIGHT INSTRUCTOR

28 December 1944

TRANSITION FLYING TRAINING CERTIFICATE

This is to certify that the following named pilot has completed the course of transition flying training as required by Army Air Force Regulation No. 50-16 and pertinent to 55th Ftr. Gp. Operational Training Unit Memoranda:

Name of Pilot___PATTON, WILLIAM W._____

Section_____I_____

Type of airplane___P-51_____

Instructor___Herman J. Schonamberg, 1st Lieut., Air Corps___

Date instruction was successfully completed_28 December 1944___

Remarks_____

_____

Millard O. Anderson
MILLARD O. ANDERSON,
1st Lieut., Air Corps,
Operations Officer.

NOTE: Original and duplicate to be signed. Original to Section Operations Files for record; duplicate to be filed in respective pilot's Individual Flight Record Nark File.

PATTON'S TRANSITION FLYING
TRAINING CERTIFICATE FOR P-51

INDIVIDUAL FLIGHT RECORD

(1) SERIAL NO. **O-758480** (2) NAME **PATTON   WILLIAM   W., JR.** (3) RANK **1s Lt.** (4) AGE **1918**

(5) PERS. CLASS **18** (6) BRANCH **Air Corps** (7) STATION **AAF F-159** ATTACHED FOR FLYING

(8) ORGANIZATION ASSIGNED **EIGHTH 3rd Bomb Div 66th Ftr 55th Ftr Hq**

(9) ORGANIZATION ATTACHED **EIGHTH 3rd Bomb Div 66th Ftr 55th Ftr O.T.U.**

(10) PRESENT RATING, & DATE **Pilot-11-9-43** (11) ORIGINAL RATING & DATE **Same**

(12) TRANSFERRED FROM **Station No. 196 APO 559** (13) FLIGHT RESTRICTIONS **None**

(15) TRANSFERRED TO **55th Ftr Gp., APO 559** (14) TRANSFER DATE **17 December 1944.**

(16)

PERS. CLASS	RANK	RTG.	A.F.	COMMAND	WING	GROUP NO.	TYPE	SQUADRON NO.	TYPE	STATION	MO. YR.	(17) MONTH **DECEMBER** , **44**

DAY	AIRCRAFT TYPE, MODEL & SERIES	NO. LANDINGS	FLYING INST. (INCL. IN 1ST PIL. TIME) S	COMMD. PILOT C CA	CO-PILOT CP	QUALI-FIED PILOT DUAL QD	FIRST PILOT DAY P	FIRST PILOT NIGHT P N DR N	RATED PERS. NON-PILOT P-AI	NON-RATED OTHER ARMS & SERVICES	NON-RATED OTHER CREW PASS OR	INSTRU-MENT ?	NIGHT N	INSTRU-MENT TRAINER	PILOT NON-MIL AIRCRAFT OVER 400 H.P.	PILOT NON-MIL AIRCRAFT UNDER 400 H.P.
18	19	20	21	22	23	24	25	26	27	28	29	30	31	32	33	34	35	36
28	P-51B	1					1:30									
31	P-51D	1					1:20									

CERTIFIED CORRECT

Millard O. Anderson

MILLARD O. ANDERSON,
1st Lieut., Air Corps,
Operations Officer.

| COLUMN TOTALS | | | | | | | 2:50 | | | | | | | | | |

	(42) TOTAL STUDENT PILOT TIME	(43) TOTAL FIRST PILOT TIME			(44) TOTAL PILOT TIME
(37) THIS MONTH		2:50			2:50
(38) PREVIOUS MONTHS THIS F.Y.		31:00			32:30
(39) THIS FISCAL YEAR		33:50			35:20
(40) PREVIOUS FISCAL YEARS	273:55	213:30	26:80		629:55
(41) TO DATE	273:55	257:20	26:10		665:15

	AIRCRAFT	NL	CARD NO. 1					CARD NO. 2					CARD NO. 3			
	19	20	21	22	23	24	25	26	27	28	29	30	31	32	33	34	35	36

FORM 5 SHOWING P-51 CHECKOUT

CHAPTER 7

SEARCH FOR COMRADES-IN-ARMS

One of my very first tasks in developing the Patton story, was to locate men who had served with him in the military. The documentation tells a story of events but does little to describe the human aspects of William Patton. For this, I needed first hand testimony from his comrades-in-arms. Thus began a Lengthy search.

THE WILLIAM W. ("PAT" / "JUNIOR" / " BILL") JR. AS THEY KNEW HIM

In reviewing the documents which I collected for this story, a definite personality emerged: One who was a "Straight-A student" exemplified by the top scores on all tests & evaluations, backed by commendations and rapid promotions in period in which time in grade could be measured in decades. This was the academic score but what of the man himself? For this I desperately needed to find comrades who actually served with him and knew his true personality.

My search bore fruit and to the man, all confirmed that William W. Patton Jr, was indeed a "Straight-A" Personality as well as being accomplished in every area of his life. It was a unanimous observation that Patton was a marvelous human being. While totally dedicated to accomplishing his military assignments as perfectly as humanly possible, he was also a true friend to all who knew him. He was truly loved by his comrades-in-arms!

SCOUTS WHO SERVED WITH PATTON

Simultaneous with a search for family members was contact with members of the 3rd Scouting Force who would remember Patton and who had flown on that final mission.

O.V. Lancaster was a 3rd Scouting Force pilot who actually flew missions with Patton on the 1st, 5th, 7th and 8th of January 1945. However, O.V. has no recollection of Patton.

Cliff Manlove was a Pilot in the 3rd Scouting Force who arrived at Wormingford about the same time as Patton but there are no indications that they flew any of the same missions.

Byron Cook was an Aerial Gunner who responded to my 388th inquiry and provided a big bonus as he had not only flown missions with the 388th but also stayed over at Wormingford to become a key Non-Commissioned Officer in the 3rd Scout Headquarters.

A review of the missions flown by the 3rd Scouts in January 1945 revealed the names of other pilots who flew with Patton but sadly, time has taken these warriors away from us. They included **LuVerne Abendroth, Tom Fitzsimons, Tony Klansinski and Ed Unger,**

OTHER MILITARY COMRADES

This phase of the search also included anyone who had served with Patton at any time during his 10 year Military career. Initial data provided by the family confirmed that he had served at Randolph Field, Texas, Hickam Field, Hawaii, numerous training bases in the US and in England with the 8th Air Force.

I launched this effort immediately with 4 actions. I prepared an article for the 8th Air Force Historical Society Quarterly; ran all of the names provided by family contact through an Internet search ;contacted the AAF Veterans Associations which represented the units in which he had served and finally, consulted all available historical documents in my possession. All efforts paid off handsomely.

5TH BOMB GROUP –HICKHAM FIELD, HAWAII

I found a number of folks who were members of the 5th Bomb Group and were stationed at Hickam In the late 30's and early 40's. They were all present during the 7 December sneak attack by the Japs and had very interesting tales to tell. These adventures are chronicled in Chapter 5. Those located included:Doug Allen – Fresno, CA, Byram Bates – Helendale, CA, Donald Bloomfield – The Village, FL, Elman F. Lemley – Naples, FL, Dick Modling – Piedmont, CA, David Miller(Wm. H. Stewart-Washington, DC) and Joe Peseck – Ovieda, FL

Charles Werntz – St. Louis, MO

I found Charles on a roster of the 5th Bomb Group members of the Pearl Harbor Survivors Association. Immediate contact was made via telephone and he provided a treasure trove of information about life at Hickam Field and about William Patton. Charles knew Patton very well as they worked together

Doug Hicks-Arlington, Texas

Doug was assigned to Coast Artillery at Pearl Harbor and early in his service met William Patton socially. The two became fast friends and shared everything including the 7 December 1941 attack by the Japanese. William was Hickam Field firing a machine gun from behind the wreckage of a B-17 while Doug was at the entrance to the harbor, firing his rifle at Japanese aircraft.

Doug and William went on to take their Aviation Cadet exams together, went thru pilot training and B-17 crew training together and went overseas together to be assigned to the 94th Bomb Group of the 8th Air Force. Unfortunately, they saw little of each other after the start of combat training and the flying of combat missions and shortly after Patton left the 94th for a Project Aphrodite assignment.

Doug responded to an article I had published in the 8th Air Force Historical Society with a telephone call. We had a wonderful conversation and when it came time to exchange addresses, **it turns out he and I only live 6 blocks apart!** As soon as this fact was revealed I grabbed my Video camera and headed to Doug's home for a wonderful 3 hour session. Doug was closer to William, for a longer period, than any other of his Comrades, thus knew him very well. Once again, Patton was Described as "the greatest".

DOUG HICKS - 1944
PATTON'S BEST FRIEND

DOUG HAS NOT CHANGED MUCH OVER THE YEARS

OTHER 5ᵀᴴ BOMB GROUP PERSONNEL

During my 5BG search, I discovered some who did not know Patton but were a delight to converse with and recall some of the memories of those dark days early in World War II. This Included **Donald Kaster-Rochester, Minnesota, Harold Nicholson-Greenville, Rhode Island, John Sandell-Moscow, Idaho and Mrs. Robert Samson-Loveland, Colorado**

Other Pilot Training Classmates

While reviewing Patton's files I came across a letter that was written to Patton by **James H. Shawhan** on 13 March 1944. A check of the Class 43-J graduating class listed a James Shawhan. I launched an Internet search and immediately found a James H. Shawhan listed in southern Indiana. A quick telephone call confirmed that Shawhan and Patton were classmates though out pilot training and had become good friends in the process. The amazing part of this contact was that the wife and I were scheduled to attend the annual Atkins family reunion in Indiana and the Shawhans live only 20 miles from the reunion site! Plans were made to meet and on 1 September 2001 the Atkins and Shawhan met for a marvelous afternoon of remembrance. Jim recalled those very pleasant training days and recalled that Patton was one of the most pleasant persons he had ever known. **Betty Shawhan** also remembered "Pat" Patton as a delightful person and a very handsome young man. The afternoon was spent in nostalgic recollections and pictures were taken to document this event. After a fine dinner together we bade farewell to return to our reunion activities. We had the opportunity to be together once again on 9 November 2001, as both families attended the Patton military service in Springfield, Missouri

While canvassing the 43-J graduating class list, I located Patton classmate **Floren Nelson** in Utah. Floren was selected for Martin B-26 bomber training. He put me in touch with Patton classmates **Maurice Neher** and **Charles O'Mahoney**, who also flew B-26's.

Aphrodite Project/388th Bomb Group

John Hinner-According to John Hinner was Patton's co-pilot on his "hot" mission. He was located but was unable to provide any information. John passed away in 2003. Wife Virginia has been a great help in filling in some blanks about John's service on the Aphrodite Project.

John Lansing-As a result of the Patton article in the 8th Air Force Historical Society newsletter I received a telephone call from John Lansing, Aphrodite project pilot. John is now retired in California.

Fain Pool - An internet search enabled me to contact Fain Pool who was in the very first group of Aphrodite pilots. He kindly permitted me to publish his own story about this most unusual experiment in early guided missilery.

JIM SHAWHAN-PATTON CLASSMATE
WITH WIFE BETTY
After Flight Training, Jim went on to fly a full combat tour
in B-17's with the 452nd Bomb Group of the 8th Air Force

Betty and Jim "Back home in Indiana"

94th Bomb Group

Immediately upon receiving Crew Load Lists for Patton's June missions and the June 1944 Pilot Roster for the 331st Bomb Squadron, I began an Internet search for all of those listed in both areas. English Aviation Historian and 8th Air Force Buff, **Anthony Plowright** acquired the data for me after all American sources had failed, once again proving that the Brits are the best when WW II heritage is at stake. Here are the names and the results to date: I was unable to account for any of Patton's regular B-17 crew except for B.F. Younginer, who had passed away in 1999. I found substitute crew members E.BV. Cassler and A.E. Soltman but neither had any memories of Patton or the other crew members.

94TH BOMB GROUP / 331ST BOMB SQUADRON PILOTS ON JUNE 1944 MISSIONS

In addition to William Patton, Crew load lists for the June missions flown by the 331st -Squadron include the following pilots; R.B. Allison, C.E. Davis, R.M. Dean, A.L. Gette J.R. Griffitt, L.D. Hicks, W.D. Jacobs, W.F. Jester, A. Manz, J.F. Moriarity, J.H. Moser, F.R. Peterson, L.F. Pursglove, R.W. Schumacher And J.R. Whorton. An Internet search was conducted and the associations of the 331st Squadron and the 94th Group were queried in an attempt to locate these gentlemen. Only **L.D. Hicks and Bob Allison** were found.

CADET BILL NEHER

BILL NEHER - 2006

**BILL NEHER AND HIS B-26
CREW WHILE IN TRAINING**

PART III

HONORS

CHAPTER 8

MEMORIALS

Lt. William W. Patton Jr. was eulogized in a funeral service in Neosho, Missouri and buried with full military honors at the Springfield, Missouri National Cemetery. He was further honored at ceremonies in France and at an air museum in Springfield.

2001 FUNERAL SERVICE IN NEOSHO

Funeral services were conducted at the Clark Funeral Home near downtown Neosho, Missouri. The chapel was filled to capacity with family, former comrades-in-arms, friends, and well wishers as well as many members of the media. The family had prepared a beautiful display of photographs and memorabilia plus a computer presentation of Lt. Pattons life.

The service was conducted by Reverend Norman Taylor. It was especially emotional for Reverend Taylor as he was the brother-in-law of Patton and had known him personally.

-+The burial took p[lace at the National Cemetery in Springfield, some 60 miles from Neosho. This turned out to be a most memorable journey. The funeral procession consisted of about 40 automobiles with a local police escort to the Neosho city limits. Because the route was on a 2 lane highway which passed through dozens of towns, the potential for delay was great because of the dozens of intersections and traffic lights along the routs. However, much to our relief, <u>every intersection in every town enroute was blocked by police</u> and the procession never slowed. When we reached the city limits of Springfield another police escort sped us thru the city and every intersection was blocked by a uniformed Springfield policeman who honored the occasion with a snappy military salute as the motorcade passed. A most inspiring entry into the city.

We later learned that the these marvelous courtesies, for the entire trip, were arranged by Kirk Manlove, son of Lt. Col. Cliff Manlove, member of Pattons 3rd Scouting Force during WW II. Kirk is Spokesman for the Springfield Police Department.

BURIAL AT THE NATIONAL SPRINGFIELD CEMETERY

The National Cemetery

Something that all Americans can view with pride is the National Cemetery system. This incredible example of what is very right with our national government, is Administered by the National Battle Monuments Commission. It provides a final resting place for our honored dead and assures a fitting memorial in tribute for their supreme sacrifice in the defense of our great country.

The Springfield site, established in 1862, is an 18 acre plot within the city limits of Springfield. It contains the honored remains from every American conflict beginning with the Civil War. Among more than 14,000 heroes interred are 4 Medal Of Honor recipients from the Civil War, World War I and World War II.

In
Honor and Remembrance
of

William Wyatt Patton, Jr.
1ᵉᵗ Lt.— U.S. Army Air Force
WWII Pilot

The long wait for William Patton Was ended on 9 november 2001 when he was returned to his final resting place in the National Cemetary in Springfield, Illinois

MARGARET PATTON

REV NORMAN TAYLOR AND JEAN PATTON MONTEZ

DONNA PATTON BROWN

JOAN TAYLOR SPEE

WILLIAM PATTON JR. LIES IN STATE

**THE PATTON FAMILY AT THE SPRINGFIELD
NATIONAL CEMETERY**

LT. COL. CLIFF MANLOVE
3RD SCOUTING FORCE
WITH WIFE JANE AND SON CRAIG

COLONEL IVAN CALTON
3RD SCOUTING FORCE

BETTY AND JIM SHAWHAN

GENERAL LACY AND MRS LACY

COMRADES IN ARMS AT PATTON FUNERAL

WILLIAM WYATT PATTON JR.
REST IN HONORED GLORY

Burial Services

Upon entering the cemetery grounds, we were greeted by a US Army Honor Guard, a large gathering of local citizens and media.

Members of the Honor Guard tenderly removed the casket and placed it on a catafalque. Reverend Taylor complete the service with the final eulogy. A 21 gun military salute by a 7 man Army team completed the services.

This was followed by the type of bittersweet reunion that often attends such occasions. Many members of the Patton family, former 3rd Scouts Colonel Ivan Calton, former 3rd Scout Lt. Colonel Cliff Manlove and Wife June plus Pilot Training Classmate Jim Shawhan and wife Betty, shared in the reunion.

SCHEDULED 2002 MEMORIAL SERVICES IN FRANCE

Memorial services were originally scheduled in France on the 15 January 2002 anniversary of Pattons death but the tragic events of 11 September induced security restrictions that forced cancellation of the event. This was a great disappointment to the French and American officials and citizens who were to attend but all understood the necessity for such action. Happily the event was rescheduled for the 2003 anniversary.

2003 MEMORIAL SERVICES IN FRANCE

No sooner was the 2002 cancellation announced than the citizens of La Longueville and Feignies, France began their planning for a 2003 event. Invitations were extended to the the all members of the French & American Diplomatic & Military establishment and Citizenry who had participated in the 2001 recovery operation, the Patton family, former members of the 3rd Scouting Force plus Scouting Force Historian and 8th Air Force Historian. The ceremonies took place on 15 January 2003 with Lt Patton's Niece, Connie Patton representing the Patton family. This was an incredible event which reflected the strong feeling that the

French citizens have for the memory of William Patton and the sacrifice that he made on behalf of the civilized world.

Connie and her friend arrived in La Longeuville on 14 January and were welcomed with open arms and treated like royalty by the local dignitaries and the citizenry. The ceremonies began on the morning of the 15th with a church service, followed by a walk to the site of the eternal flame. The streets were lined with hundreds of citizens of all ages, there to honor the fallen warrior thru his kin. Connie lighted the flame while the throngs looked on in reverent silence.

The group then motored to Fort Leveau in Feignies for an additional ceremony and then toured the museum.

This was a very emotional experience for all.........tears of sadness and joy flowed.

**SERVICES AT CHURCH
IN LA LONGUEVILLE -2003**

CONNIE PATTON AT MEMORIAL CEREMONY IN 2003

DIGNITARIES AND CITIZENS GATHER FOR FORMAL OPENING OF THE PATTON MUSEUM AT FORT LEVEAU

2005 MEMORIAL SERVICES IN FRANCE

Another memorial service was conducted in January 2005. Again, Connie Patton attended and was again was accompanied by her friend Tammy Haddock. The ceremonies took place on the 15th of January 2005, the 60th anniversary of the death of William Patton.

As in the previous events, the citizens of the La Longueville- Feignies-Maubeuge area feted the girls in grand style and displayed the typical French hospitality in a mood of sincere reverence for the memory of the fallen hero.

(L TO R) PHILLIPE DHUYVETTERE, FRANCINE LEMAITTE, CECILE LEMAITTE, TAMMY HADDOCK, GILLES ROSERENS, CONNIE PATTON, CLAUDE LEMAITTE, LINDA MCINTOSH, STEVE MCINTOSH AND RICHARD HUCKABY

GATHERING AT THE PATTON GRAVESITE MEMORIAL IN LALONGUEVILLE FRANC- JANUARY 2005

2005 MUSEUM DEDICATION IN SPRINGFIELD

The family had been working through their local Congressman, Representative Roy Blunt, since 2002 to bring portions of the Patton Mustang wreckage to the United States. Concurrently, the Air and Military Museum of Springfield had offered space to display these artifacts honoring a native son.

After considerable negotiations between the US and French governments and extensive arrangements with customs officials, aircraft artifacts were delivered to the museum. The Patton family also donated personal effects of Lt. Patton including the shirt and tie he wore during the fatal mission. A large oil painting of Lt. Patton, by Texas Artist George Kloepfer, was jointly donated to the museum by Scout Historian E. Richard Atkins and Artist Kloepfer. On 16 August 2005, the artifacts and Painting were dedicated in a moving ceremony.

CONNIE PATTON AND CLIFF MANLOVE AT PRESENTATION OF WILLIAM W. PATTON JR. PORTRAIT

William Patton's sister-in-law, Margaret Patton and nieces Connie Patton, Donna Patton Brown and Joyce Patton Montez represented the Patton family while Lt. Col. Cliff Manlove stood in for the 3rd Scouting Force.

Guest of honor was Congressman Roy Blunt, who had done so much in aiding the Patton family through the entire traumatic journey of identification, returning Lt. Patton home, the burial and gaining access to the Mustang parts.

CONGRESSMAN BLUNT (R-MO) AND CLIFF MANLOVE AT PATTON PORTRAIT PRESENTATION – BLUNT WAS A MAJOR FACTOR IN BRINGING PATTON HOME.

CHAPTER 9

BUILDING THE MUSEUM
IN FRANCE

Once William Patton was found, many in France and the United States began considering memorials to this long lost airman. The French almost immediately established a museum near the crash site

Upon discovery of the wreckage of Junior's Mustang, the citizens of Feignies, La Longeuville and adjacent communities became deeply involved. The French are normally emotional people but this was a very special case which reached deep into the hearts of all. First, these communities lie within some of the most sacred ground in France, the battlefields of World War I. Land which is stained with the blood of countless brave French soldiers as well as its citizens of both World Wars. Secondly, the crash site stands in the very shadows of Fort de Leveau, a World War I fortification which was shelled by the Germans early in the conflict and in which the remains of many French soldiers were entombed. Finally, the thought of a gallant comrade-in-arms, lying buried for 56 years at their very doorstep, became a heavy burden to all of these patriotic folks. All of this brought forth a desire to provide a permanent memorial to William Wyatt Patton Junior.

What more fitting place to honor this fallen airman than the fortress itself, which already contained a museum in honor of the 1914 French comrades-in-arms; and that they did. With loving care they prepared a fortress room and placed in it wreckage of Patton's P-51 Mustang, some of his personal flight gear and associated materials befitting such a memorial.

For my part, I provided a plaque in Junior's memory and 2 copies of my book, "Fighting Scouts of the 8th Air Force," one copy for reviewing by visitors and a second for display. The photos show what great care was exercised to assure an honored remembrance.

As in all endeavors, leadership and dedicated workers are the key to success. In this case Guillaume LaMaitte spearheaded the effort. He was supported by a group of young aviation enthusiasts and historians from the area. With the blessing of the city officials and the encouragement of all local citizens, the group launched this labor of love.

Beginning with a bare room formed of concrete blocks, the group set about to completely remodel the space. They first fabricated wood frames to form the shape of the room. These frames were secured to the walls and the ceiling. The frame was then covered with wallboard, plastered and painted. The next task was to build a steel tube framework to hold the wreckage of Patton's Mustang with parts in the proper special relationship to each other. With the parts mounted, the next task was the addition of wall displays and display cases with small artifacts. Every phase of the construction was pursued with loving care in reverence to him who was honored there.

The lads worked hard to meet the 15 January 2002 deadline for the first annual Patton memorial gathering And they did meet it…with spectacular results.

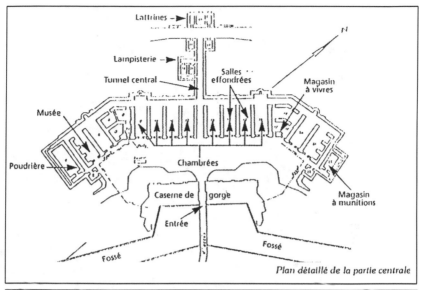

Lattrines

Lampisterie

Tunnel central

Salles effondrées

Musée

Magasin à vivres

Poudrière

Chambrées

Caserne de gorge

Entrée

Magasin à munitions

Fossé

Fossé

Plan détaillé de la partie centrale

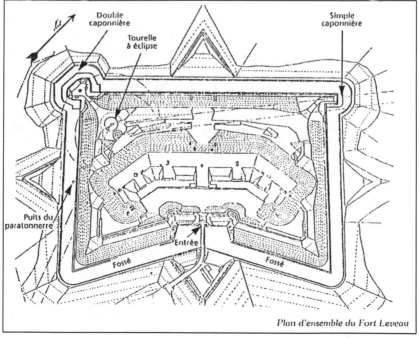

Double caponnière

Simple caponnière

Tourelle à éclipse

Puits du paratonnerre

Entrée

Fossé

Fossé

Plan d'ensemble du Fort Leveau

PLAN OF FORT DE LAVEAU

FORT DE LAVEAU VIEWED FROM AIR AND GROUND

**GILLAUME LEMAITTE LEADS VOLUNTEERS
IN BUILDING PATTON MUSEUM**

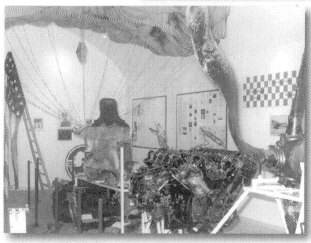

**THE COMPLETED MUSEUM
A FITTING TRIBUTE**

CHAPTER 10

THE SCOUTING FORCE

From the beginning of operations in mid-1942, the 8ᵗʰ Bomber Command was primarily concerned with the Command, Logistics and Personnel Problems that plague a new force launching into combat operations. All thoughts were directed toward dealing with the enemy in the form of flack and fighters. They were soon to learn that there was another enemy: the weather! The 3ʳᵈ Scouting Force was William Patton's final military assignment.

WILLIAM PATTON

As noted in previous chapters, Patton's tour in the Scouting Force lasted only 15 days. In the fashion which was typical of this young warrior, his flight records attest to the fact that he spent every available moment in his Mustang, learning the procedures and processes of Scouting. This to assure that he always produced a quality effort. This left him little time to become acquainted with members of his unit, thus we have no living witnesses to tell his story. But we do know from evidence of previous service that he was surely as dedicated to the scouting mission and did his very best right up to the final flight!

THE OPERATIONAL IMPACT OF WEATHER

Inclement weather, in the form of cloud formations, thunderstorms, rain, sleet, snow, ice, wind and fog can impact flight operations in every phase. Taxiing and takeoff can be difficult and dangerous; Assembly of the Flight, Squadron, Group, Wing and the Mission Task Force may be delayed and is an arena for possible mid-air collisions. The greater the number of aircraft the greater the danger of collisions, even in clear weather. Going to the target and finding the target can be severely compromised. Many 8th Air Force missions were rendered unsuccessful because of bad weather. Until radar bombing equipment was developed, more missions were aborted or unsuccessful because of bad weather than for any other cause. Weather can adversely affect the flight home and the approach and landing can be rendered lethal by bad weather.

EARLY WEATHER RECONNAISSANCE

The answer to the question of just how big a factor the weather can be, came during the first winter and efforts to improve forecasting quality were launched. The 18th Weather Squadron began weather surveys in September 1943. They provided weather observers to fly weather reconnaissance missions in aircraft with crews provided by various bomb groups. Although useful, the full value could not be attained because the flights were limited to friendly skies. In March 1944, the mission was taken over by the 8th Weather Reconnaissance Service which ultimately became the 652nd Bomb Squadron of the 25th Bomb Group. In addition to their stripped down B-17's and B-24's, Speedy Mosquito Bombers, obtained from the British, were used to extend the weather sorties over the Continent. This provided the weather specialists improved and more timely information with which to prepare their forecasts.

THE FORECASTING CHALLANGE

The problem lay in the fact that all efforts were pointed toward forecasting. Forecasting may be described as an "educated guess." The

<u>educated</u> portion comes in the scientific knowledge of the professional combined with the best available information provided by all data gathering apparatus. The guess represents the forecast based on the combination of expertise and data. In those early years of Military Meteorology, It was a crap shoot any time but in this part of the world the odds, especially in the winter months, are stacked against the weather forecaster. The reason: the tools were just not sophisticated enough and the weather changes too rapidly. Under the best of conditions, the forecast could be 4 to 6 hours old by the time the bomber stream is enroute and can reach the target. Major changes can take place in far less time. In the winter this was the rule rather than the exception. To top it all, the height, width and depth of any cloud group could not be predicted. You simple had to be there to know what you faced at any given time. The weather folks gave their all but it just wasn't enough to satisfy the beleaguered bomber commanders.

The first 8th Air Force weather reconnaissance began in September 1943 with members of the 18th Weather Squadron. They were assigned temporary duty flying weather reconnaissance. On 28 March 1944, weather reconnaissance became the responsibility of the 25th Bomb Group's 652nd and 653rd Squadrons stationed at Watton, England. The 652nd was equipped with the B-17G and B-24D and H aircraft. These aircraft were heavily modified with additional fuel tanks, all weapons and armor removed and the nose interior revised and equipped for the weather observer.

3 separate daily missions were scheduled. The first flight had a triangular path with the 1st leg some 800 miles out over the Atlantic Ocean, a 120 degree turn and several hundred miles on the 2nd leg with the final 120 turn taking them back to Watton. The 2nd mission was along the coast of Europe and then to the Azores. The following day this airplane returned to Watton from the Azores. Flying these missions provided an average of 1.5 aircraft in the air, 24 hours per day for some 13 months!

During each of these 3 missions weather readings were taken every 50 miles at altitudes ranging from 30,000 feet down to 50 feet. The 652nd flew a total of 1270 weather missions with an average flight time of 12.1 hours per mission. They suffered the loss of 6 of their unarmed B-17 and B-24 aircraft, all in operational missions. In all, an outstanding piece of work.

The 653rd Squadron was equipped with the British DeHavilland Mosquito Mark PR.XVI. This 2 place, plywood "hotrod" was ideally suited for the Recon mission. Its two 1290 horsepower Merlin engines could push it along at over 400 miles per hour. It could outrun any American or German fighter. With A range of over 1800 miles it was indeed a formidable little airplane. The "Mossie", as it known by the operators, were primarily concentrated over the Continent and provided rapid turnaround of weather data. These weather flights were code named "Bluestocking" and the data was available to all Allied forces. Some 1131 "Bluestocking" flights were made by the 653rd during their 13 months of operations.

BUDD PEASLEE KNEW THE PROBLEM

As a veteran Bomber Pilot and Bomber Group Commander, Scouting Force originator Col. Budd Peaslee knew first hand that the "bombers needed eyes." He had led his beloved 384th Bomb Group on some of the toughest missions of the war in the bitter days of 1943.

The 384th had been to Halberstadt, Magdeburg and the infamous "Black Thursday" Schweinfurt raid when there was no fighter escort, just enemy flack and fighters. As a soldier, he knew his job was to confront the enemy and do his best to kill them. The thing that frustrated Budd the most was the one enemy that he was helpless to defeat; the weather. He had experienced the ever changing conditions in central Europe and the havoc wreaked on mission, man and machine. Like all those who felt the wrath of Mother Nature, he knew that something should and could be done about it. When Budd became passionate about something, things happened.

THE MISSION THAT SPARKED SCOUTING

The mission that really brought the problem to the boiling point in Col. Peaslee's mind was flown on 29 June 1943 which He described in the February 1957 issue of Flying Magazine. It went like this:

"On the morning in question I sat in the pilot's seat of my B-17 at 25,000 feet as we approached the English Channel from the West. Behind in formation stretched the bomber stream.We had assembled in perfect weather over our bases and were set for the penetration of Nazi defenses on the Continent. We had been carefully briefed to destroy a major military objective deep in occupied France. Our briefing contained repeated warnings on operations over occupied countries for those people were our friends, temporarily in the hands of an invader. It was accepted by us and them that we would occasionally hurt them in our efforts to destroy Hitler's facilities in their homeland. But, we would keep the destruction to a minimum. If we ere not able to make a good, clean run on the target we would bring our bombs back to England. Our one exception from such restrictions was an occupied German Airdrome.

As we reached the English Channel a wall of clouds, conforming almost exactly to the French coastline, arose between us, unbroken except for a narrow canyon between the towering Cumulus clouds immediately ahead. What should I do? Should I lead the 8th Bomber Command into this narrow defile and take a chance on being able to maneuver the clumsy formations once I had committed them? Would the corridor between the clouds open up beyond? Would we be able to get behind the more distant cloud barrier? I would have given anything to know what lay beyond my immediate vision. I knew that if I had to turn my formation (1st section of the 1st Bomb Wing) in the cloud canyon we would be forced into the Cumlulus; that with all of those bombers flying formation on instruments there would be inevitable collisions with loss of life and equipment. Just short of the cloud barrier I made my decision-to abort the mission.

As I swung into my 180 degree turn, always the undecided pilot's best maneuver, I noted the bomber division (second section of the 1st Bomb

Wing) behind me was following my lead; I also noted that the third bomber division (4th Bomb Wing)was plunging ahead into the canyon. As I led my fomation back to England I broke into a sweat. It is a tremendous responsibility to reverse the orders of a superior in war. It would not have been so bad if the third division had followed my lead for then we would never have known whether I erred in Judgment. If they got through to the target I would perhaps, be relieved of command. All the way back I was trying to solve my problem. Had I been able to talk to someone scouting my route beyond the cloud wall, what a relief it would have been. Just one fighter plane out there with a radio could have told me what to do. But I didn't have one. Our fighters of that period couldn't do the job because of their limited range. So here we were in the 8th Bomber Command, committing a tremendous force to battle without route reconnaissance. Not even ground armies moved into action without reported detail of what lay in their path. We had nothing but an ancient map.

These thoughts were running thru my mind time after time during the return flight. The third division did get thru the wall of clouds and bombed *the target but not the one they had been briefed for; it was covered with clouds!* Col. Peaslee was off the hook!

This mission had lit Colonel Peaslees fire on the subject of scouting. Over the next few months he had a series of discussions with other Bomb Group commanders about the weather problem and the idea of a fighter scouting ahead. They related situations far worse than Budd had experienced including unexplained loss of bombers and incoming formations meeting outgoing formations head-on. They were all for the scouting idea.

THE SCOUTING CONCEPT TAKES SHAPE

The problem of a suitable airplane still remained. The Dehavilland Mosquito had the neccessary range and speed but the AAF didn't have any and they were in limited supply in the RAF. Besides, Budd had his eyes on the P-51 Mustang which was replacing the P-38's and P-47's. His logic was correct in selecting the Mustang. Fast enough, with adequate range to reach any target. Able to defend itself and a relatively easy airplane to fly, it was the ideal steed for the job.

Equally important were the men who would fly those fighters. He knew the ideal Aviators to perform the scouting misson; experienced bomber pilots, who understood the fundamental problem facing the bombers; SLOW AIRPLANES AND FAST WEATHER. He knew that most good bomber pilots would love to fly a fighter and banked on that fact to get the right volunteers and they had to be volunteers if a quality effort was to result.

There were two critical elements which made his scouting concept destined for success. First, was the fact that bomber pilot's could fly safely in the worst of weather. They were trained and highly experienced in the art of instrument flying, a skill very few of their fighter counterparts possessed. Second, his use of multiple aircraft in recognition of the fact most missions were planned for multiple targets and the scouting force needed flexibility to deal with the tactical decisions made enroute to the target(s), which often split the bomber forces.

COLONEL BUDD GOES INTO ACTION

With his tour as the 384th Bomb Group Commander complete and the Scouting Force concept well in mind, Budd began lobbying higher headquarters to make the concept a reality. He first went to General Kepner, who commanded all fighter resources in the 8th Air Force, and convinced him that scouting was a sound idea. Budd was then assigned to 8th Air Force headquarters to work with Col Robert Burns, Operations Chief of the 8th Fighter Command. Budd prepared the Operations Plan and set about to implement the plan.

Fate intervened when Budd was assigned as Liaison Officer between the 8th and 15th Air Forces for 90 days. In his absence the plan had gone no place for lack of a point man. Budd returned to England from Italy, where he was working with General Twining's 15th Air Force staff, and settled into a new job as Deputy Commander of the 40th Combat Wing under Col. Howard Turner. He immediately revived the scouting plan and sold Col. Turner who recommended that he take it to General Bob Williams, 1st Air Division Commander. General Williams heartily endorsed it to General Doolittle, 8th Air Force Commander. Col. Peaslee had the opportunity to personally brief General Doolittle who sent him to brief the 2nd and 3rd Air division Commanders, Generals Partridge and Lemay. They both approved and Budd was on his way.

IMPLEMENTING THE SCOUTING PLAN

He returned to 8th Air Force headquarters where General Doolittle's staff where action was taken to implement Budd's plan thru the selection of a supporting Fighter Group, selection of pilots, acquisition of aircraft, establishment of logistics support, preparing for training and development of the operations plan. There were 2 stipulations by General Doolittle. First, the Scouting force must go thru a trial period to prove its worth and the organization would not be a permanent force with Table of Organization and Equipment authorization but, would be a provisional unit. The first stipulation was understandable and fully accepted by Col. Peaslee. The second was a bitter disappointment for it meant that the scouting mission had a temporary air about it and no one could be promoted within the unit. Any advancements must come from the home squadron and that was unlikely. (The 1st Scouting Force did finally become a TO&E Organization as the 857 Bomb Squadron in March 1945 as did the 3rd Scouting Force which became the 862nd Bomb Squadron). Being the good soldier that he was and realizing the importance of the mission, Budd proceeded to create the Experimental Scouting Force. 8th Air Force Planners agreed with Budd's request to authorize 8 bomber pilots from Lead crews, a Deputy Commander, Navigator, Intelligence Officer, Operations Officer with Fighter Pilots to be furnished by the supporting Fighter Group. The Scouting force was finally on its way!

THE SCOUTING FORCE (EXPERIMENTAL) Once Col. Peaslee had received General Doolittle's permission to service test a Scouting Force, he wasted no time in getting the operation going. He began at once with the Operations planning, logistics development and acquisition of personnel and equipment.

THE HOST GROUP - Testimony from all who knew Bud Peaslee identified him as a man of action, who detested "paper work." As a result, documentation covering the Scouting Force (Experimental) is practically non-existent. The fact that the organization had no personnel other than Pilots and a few Operations personnel and depended upon the 355th Fighter Group for all administration, sealed the bargain. This greatly pleased Colonel Peaslee and his pilots but makes life very difficult for historians attempting to document the history of the Scouts.

The 355th Fighter Group at Steeple Morden was selected as the host group for the Scouting experiment. Arrangements were made by Col Peaslee with Col. William J. Cummings Jr., the Group Commander, to provide aircraft, logistics support and Fighter Pilots. The Scouts made up what was essentially a 4th Squadron. This activity took place about the middle of June 1944. Colonel Cummings assigned his Deputy Commander, Lt.Col. Everett Stewart as liaison between the 355th and the Scouts. This was indeed, a very fortunate choice for both the Scouts and the Fighter group because the task at hand was a very difficult one, calling for a great deal of coordination, diplomacy and tact; Col. Stewart had plenty of each.

The challenge that faced both organizations was set in motion by 8th Air Force headquarters in its direction of the Scouting Force operation. First, the 355th, which already had it's hands full in accomplishing the fighter mission, suddenly found itself with a squadron-size tenant unit for which it had to furnish housing, food, administration, supplies, security, 8 of it's precious P-51D aircraft and all of the personnel to maintain them! To add to the burden, Col. Cummings had NO Command control. Col.Peaslee reported directly to the Commanding General of the 1st Air Division! This could have been an explosive situation but for the patience of Bill Cummings and the diplomacy of Everett Stewart. To the credit of all, it was a smooth operation from the very beginning.

MISSION SUMMARY-SCOUTING FORCE (EXP) JULY-SEPTEMBER 1944

Unfortunately, no official summary of SFX Operations could be located, however, reviewing individual Combat Logs indicates a total of 35 missions between 16 July-18 September 1944 by the Scouting Force (Experimental). It would appear that this was the duration of the experiment and that all following missions were credited to the First Scouting Force (1SF). A compilation of data from these records confirms the following missions.

SF(Exp) Missions flown from Steeple Morden (F-122)

Mission	8BCFO	Date	Target
1	476	16 July	Munich
2	482	19 July	Munich-Augsburg
3	484	20 July	Leipzig
4	486	21 July	Schweinfurt
5	501	28 July	Mersberg
6	503	29 July	Mersberg
7	507	31 July	Munich-Ludwigshaven
8	508	1 Aug	Chatres-Melun-Orleans
9	510	2 Aug	Paris
10	512	3 Aug	Saarbrucken-Strausburg
11	514	4 Aug	Peenamunde-Anklam
12	519	5 Aug	Hannover-Langenhagen
13	524	6 Aug	Berlin
14	527	7 Aug	Bordeaux-Toulouse
15	530	8 Aug	Caen

16	533	9 Aug	Augsburg
17	541	11 Aug	Brest
18	545	12 Aug	Paris-Metz
19	548	13 Aug	Rouen
20	552	14 Aug	Metz-Stuttgart
21	554	15 Aug	Frankurt-Cologne
22	556	16 Aug	Leipzig
23	561	18 Aug	Liege-Brussells
24	568	24 Aug	Mersberg-Leipzig
25	570	25 Aug	Peenamunde-Anklam
26	575	26 Aug	Ruhr Valley
27	583/584	27 Aug	Berlin
28	595	1 Sept	Ludwigshaven
29	601	3 Sept	Ludwigshaven
30	605	5 Sept	Ludwigshaven
31	611	8 Sept	Ludwigshaven
32	613	9 Sept	Ludwigshaven
33	619	10	Sept Stuttgart
34	623	11 Sept	Mersburg
35	626	12 Sept	Ruhland-Brug

GOOD VIBES FROM 8TH AIR FORCE HEADQUARTERS

8th Air Force Headquarters now begin to think in terms of a Scouting Force for each of the 3 Air Divisions even before completion of the Experiment, as evidenced by a 17 August 1944 HQ8AF Memo from Col. Robert B. Landry to Col. Walter E. Todd, Deputy Chief-of-Staff for Operations in which he stated: "The establishment of a Scouting Force in each Division has been determined to be a requirement which is highly desirable. I believe a unit should be provided for this purpose in order that personnel with grades and ratings, aircraft and equipment can be made available. A Squadron organization seems to be about the size of the unit desired for the Scouting Force. Recommend that one

Group in each Fighter Wing be designated a 4 Squadron group as a means of providing a Scouting Force for each Division."

8TH AIR FORCE BLESSES THE SCOUTING CONCEPT

In spite of a rough start, it quickly became evident to 8th Air Force Headquarters what Budd Peaslee had known all along; the Scouting Force concept worked! The reports were flowing in from bomber commanders confirming the increased effectiveness of the bomber force thru Scouting Force assistance. Obviously the "Boss," Jimmy Doolittle, Commanding General of the 8th Air Force was convinced. On 6 September 1944 message D-69297 was transmitted to 8th Fighter Command and all of the 8th Air Force bomber units with the following directions:

*"In order to provide units in Fighter Command to perform Scouting functions for each Bomb Division, the following action will be taken: Fighter Command will submit to this Headquarters the designation of Fighter Groups to be charged with this function for each Bomb Division. Each Bomb Division will submit names of Bombardment Pilots they desire transferred to their respective Fighter groups which will perform scouting functions. Only 6 additional aircraft will be maintained in each of the Fighter Groups for this purpose until after P-38 Groups and one P-47 Groups are converted. If at that time sufficient **P-51** aircraft are available, Fighter Groups charged with scouting will be augmented to limit of availability of aircraft"*

General Kepner, Commander of the 8th Fighter Command responded the following day with message 070930B which stated that the 364th Fighter Group at Honington (F-375) would be home for the 1st Scouting Force, the 355FG at Steeple Morden (F-122) would host the 2nd scouting Force and the 55th Fighter Group at Wormingford (F-159) would support the 3rd Scouting Force. The quick turnaround of messages would indicate that a lot of coordination activity had taken place prior to General Doolittle's message. The Scouting Force was now an official 8th Air Force entity!

THE THIRD SCOUTING FORCE

The 3rd Scouting Force (3SF) was formed as a provisional organization at Wormingford, England in August 1944 under the Command of Major Vincent W. Masters. The unit achieved the formal organizational status in February as the 862nd Bomb Squadron. 140 missions were completed between September 1944 and April 1945. The 3SF was supported by the 55th Fighter Group during its entire tour.

GENESIS OF THE 3RD SCOUTING FORCE

One of the key figures in formation of the Scouting Forces and prime mover in the 3rd Air Division was Major Merrill J. Klein of the 385th Bomb Group. Major Klein, who was Operations Officer of the 549th Bomb Squadron, was keenly aware of the need for Weather and Target information, having participated in some of the toughest missions of the war.

He and good friend Major Vince Masters, 385BG lead pilot, had often discussed the advantages that could be gained with scouting capability. On 21 May 1944, Major Klein put action to these thoughts in an official letter to General Earl Partridge, Commander of the 3rd Air Division. He requested that several of the lead Fighters on each mission be flown by Bomber Pilots who could report the weather and target information to the Bomber Force.

3rd Air division approved of the plan and forwarded the request to 8th Air Force headquarters, which approved of the scouting idea but not the method recommended. In their 1 June 1944 Endorsement to Major Klein's letter, 8th Air Force, without comment, authorized one Mosquito per Air Division for scouting purposes effective 30 May 1944! The Mosquitos were apparently ineffective in the Scouting role, at least as far as Klein was concerned, as he continued to lobby for the use of Fighters as the prime vehicle. No evidence could be located that these aircraft were ever delivered to the Groups or ever flew a mission. Having moved to a new position in 3rd Air Division headquarters, he intensified his efforts. A short time later Bud Peaslee got permission from General Doolittle to form the Scouting Force(Experimental) and the die was cast for the 3rd Division. In a visit to 3AD Headquarters on 25 July 1944, engineered by Major Klein, Colonel Peaslee provided the evidence of successful scouting operations that clinched the final decision. General Partridge went immediately to General Doolittle who approved the idea for the 3rd Air Division

General Partridge sought Major Klein's counsel on a leader for the newly authorized 3rd Scouts. The choice was an easy one: Major Vince Masters, whom Klein knew to be a superb Airman and Leader, as well as a good friend. Major Masters was just completing his 28th and final mission when the opportunity was presented. Like all other Bomber Pilots who flew with the Scouts, he had always wanted to fly Fighters; as a leader, he had always wanted to command. It is an understatement to say that he jumped at the chance!

At a 3rd Air Division conference on 3 August 1944 a formal plan for the 3rd Scouting Force was adopted. It was agreed that it would be, in effect, the 4th Squadron of the 55th Fighter Group at Wormingford (Station F-159) but would report directly to the 3rd Air Division. The plan called for 55th Headquarters Squadron to furnish Quarters & Rations and Administrative support. Although not stated in the original plan, the 55th also furnished service & maintenance for the 3SF aircraft. The 66th Fighter Wing was tasked with providing 8 Fighter Pilots to support the Scout Pilots, 16 Crew chiefs to support the aircraft and an Operations Officer to direct training of the Bomber Pilots.

LT COL VINCENT W MASTERS 3RD SCOUTING FORCE COMMANDER (DR VINCE MASTERS)

LT. COLONEL VINCENT W. MASTERS
3rd Scouting Force Commander

3rd SCOUTING FORCE INTELLIGENCE OFFICER, LT. SPENCE, BRIEFS PILOTS FOR MISSION

TRAINING BEGINS

On 7 August 1944, Major Vince Masters reported to the Fighter Training Center at Goxhill (Station F-345) for some AT-6 time and checkout in the P-51 Mustang. The call had gone out throughout the 3rd Division Bomb Groups for pilots, from lead crews who had finished or were near the end of their tour, to volunteer for the scouts. These pilots were screened for basic qualifications and 7 were selected. They were ordered to Goxhill for their fighter training. By the end of August 1944, the 3SF cadre Pilot cadre had completed their initial Training and reported to Wormingford. This group included:

o Capt.Stanley E.Gagon 447BG
o Capt Andrew W.Fuller 486BG
o Capt Donald B. Gutherie 486BG
o Capt Herbert B. Howard 100BG
o Cap Orvid B. Lancaster 385BG
o 1/Lt Wm A. Sandblom 486BG
o 2/Lt Laverne Abendroth 486BG
o 2/Lt Westley G. Lundholm 100BG

In addition to the pilots, the 3SF initial cadre included Captain Ed Grabowski, Lead Navigator from the 385th Bomb group, and Captain Pat Doyle, Intelligence Officer from the 384th Bomb group. By the end of August 1944, the Third Scouting Force was fully assembled and entered into a rigorous training program. By mid-September they were pronounced combat ready and on 15 September, proceeded to complete their very first mission.

THIRD SCOUTING FORCE OPERATIONAL CONCEPT

Ed Beaty recalls 3rd Scouting Force operations were conducted as follows:

The 3rd Scouting Force flew two primary fighter missions, Kodak Yellow and Kodak Red. Kodak Yellow was a non-combat operation (did not cross into enemy territory) although often, because of weather and equipment used, it was as difficult at times, as the Kodak Red mission. Kodak White usually two ships, one of which was airborne, helped the Division Commander get his bomber stream together over and departing England. Yellow could move swiftly around talking to various group leaders, advise proximities and possible headings to get into proper formation within the division. Also, he would alert the Division leader on turns which might help the stream make up. Usually White was well out over the North Sea or across the channel before finishing its job. It did not usually carry tanks, would some times be a "slow time" engine change aircraft. Often had a bad weather recovery so it had its own hazards. I recall frequent "Thank You, Kodak White" comments from Division and Group leaders so believe that these "unsung" mission did some good at times to expedite assembly of large formations. Kodak Red was our primary mission. Normally two flights of 4 ships each was used. For multiple targets or short range operations it might be one flight. Tony Klasinski, said that one day everyone else was on a mission or away and Division needed a sudden Kodak Red on another target., he did it with one ship. His information to the bomber leader enabled a change to another IP which permitted visual bombing.

Kodak Red had three primary duties: Information on enroute weather at bomber formation altitude; cloud and smoke obscuration in IP and target areas; and any apparent indications of enemy activity in the target area. Information would be passed to the Division stream leader. Depending on fuel, Kodak Red would stay in the area to observe results and provide escort to the bombers as long as possible.

COMBAT RECORD OF THE 3RD SCOUTS

Accompanied by 8 Fighters from the 55th Fighter Group, the 3rd Scouting Force launched its first mission on 15 September 1944. With Commander Vince Masters flying lead, 8 Scouts launched for a mission to Warsaw, Poland, in support of 110 B-17's on Project FRANTIC VI. This was an effort to drop supplies to the Polish revolutionaries who were battling the Germans in an ill fated attempt to liberate Warsaw. Unfortunately, a severe weather front over the North Sea forced the mission to be recalled less than an hour after takeoff.

On this very first effort for the Scouts, they proved their worth by searching out a safe route through the front but finding none, turned the bombers back before they could enter these dangerous conditions. It was a big disappointment for the bombers but the worth of the Scouting Force concept was proven on the very first mission. The 3rd Scouts, in their Mustangs, went on to fly a total of 140 missions between 15 September 1944 and 21 April 1945. This included over 1600 sorties which made an incalculable contribution to the 3rd Air Division bomber operational success.

6 members of the 3rd Scouts, were killed in action while accomplishing these critical 8th Air Force combat missions. In addition to Patton, This included Bryan Booker, Tom Fitzsimons, Robert Hall, James Reed and John Stein.

THE B-17'S ARRIVE

Until February 1945, the 3rd Scouting Force was a P-51 Fighter outfit, co-existing with a Fighter Group, the 55th, at a Fighter Base, Wormingford. On the morning of 17 February 1945, the scene changed as a Squadron of B'17's descended upon Wormingford to become a part of the 3rd Scouting Force. The aircraft and the crews manning them were from the 862nd Bomb Squadron of the 493rd Bomb Group at Debach. At the time, Commander Vince Masters was in the United States on Rest and Recuperation Leave and Deputy Commander Stan Gagon was in charge of the 3SF. In an interview with the author in 1982, Stan stated that the arrival of the B-17's was a complete surprise to him and that he had no inkling of the action from 3rd Air Division Headquarters. Needless to say it was a bit of a shock to Stan and all of the other Third Scouts who thought they had left bombers behind when they departed their parent bomb groups. It was an even bigger shock to 55th Fighter Group Commander Colonel George T. Crowell to see Fortresses mingling with Mustang's on the taxiways and runways and in the crowded airspace around Wormingford.

Although we have no written evidence to support the contention, it is suspected that Colonel Crowell lost little sleep over the situation since he turned over command of the 55th to Lt. Col. Elwyn C. Righetti less than a week after the B-17's arrived. Righetti, having just arrived from the US and from the Training Command, probably turned the problem over to his Deputy and set about checking out in the P-51 and looking forward to air combat. It was a most interesting situation.

Dave Mullen of the 486th Bomb Group, was one of the B-17 pilots assigned to the 3rd Scouting Force. He arrived complete with aircraft and crew on 1 February 1945. He relates a few anecdotes about that period. "Our B-17's were stripped of all armament and as a result, handled like fighters. We were selected lead crews (with one exception, me) so I guess we were considered pretty good flyers.

All the P-51's made fighter peel-ups when landing so we did the same. We had a lot of fun doing that until Stan Gagon called us in and reminded us that we were there because we were outstanding pilots but please stop the fighter peel-ups before landing. If some Wheel from headquarters saw a B-17 flown like that it would be my butt, or words to that effect. Dave remembers that "On another occasion, we went to Belfast, Ireland and not having been there before, became confused about where to land because there were 2 airfields right near each other. We called the tower and asked if they had a B-24 landing and when they replied in the affirmative, we followed the B-24 in. Once on the runway we asked for taxi instructions and were rewarded by a British voice which replied, I say old boy, you are on the wrong airfield. They gave us directions and we departed Belfast but not before taking on some British female troops.

It was a lovely trip as Tom Kelly, my copilot and myself, each had a lovely lady on our lap for the trip back home. Good thing we had a reliable Autopilot." "Later we had the opportunity to land on another British Airfield but this one had grass runways. After completing our business we called the tower for takeoff instructions and got the reply,

Yank, you are cleared to rustle on the green and scramble. Tom Kelly was mystified by that reply and asked for clarification. The reply came back: OK Yanks, line up and take off." "One of our mission was to meet the B-17's and B-24's and report the enrooted weather to headquarters. We met the bomber stream in the middle of the North Sea but made no radio contact. We flew in a big circle around them. We laughed when we thought of these guys at mission debrief when they told about the B-17 circling the formation."

Ed Beaty recalls that the B-17 operations went something like this: "My memory of the 3rd Scouting Force B-17 scouting missions is limited as they operated and were briefed separately. One bomber was equipped as an airborne communications station and would fly in the vicinity of the bomb line(front) to aid England-over continent communications. The others flew specific weather recon assignments from division." Unfortunately, we have no record of the B-17 Scout missions.

THE FINAL MONTH OF 3RD SCOUT OPERATIONS

The final month of the war proved to be an eventful and costly one for the 3rd Scouting Force. While completing 17 missions in this final month of the conflict, the 3rd Scouting Force lost 3 pilots; John Stein, James Reed and Tom Fitzsimmons. The most sobering aspect of these tragedies was the fact that 2 were claimed by "Friendly Fire." They were shot down by allied personnel.

John Stein is lost

On 3 April 1945, the first victim became Lt. John Stein of Portland, Oregon when he was shot down by an unidentified American fighter. The mission was to Kiel, Germany.

Mission Flight Leader, Lt. William T. Searby wrote the following report concerning this tragedy:

"While on a weather scouting mission in the vicinity of Keil, my flight was bounced by a flight of friendly fighters. While diving away from an attacking pane I noticed Lt. Stein's airplane in a flat spin at 14,000 feet. The right wing came off and the plane continued to spin on down and went into a cloud at 11,000 feet. At this point I lost contact with the plane. It appeared not to be on fire and the canopy was intact indicating that Lt. Stein was still in the plane. I did not see the plane crash."

Kenneth Bope was also on that flight. He remembers:

"One P-51 mission with the Scouts on a day when the weather was less than favorable over Denmark, remains clearly in my mind today. We were mistakenly identified by other (American) fighters in the area. Aware of their presence and satisfied as to their identy, we went on about our business and were suprised by a lone attacker who shot down my right wingman, John Stein. Taking evasive action, one of my wing tanks was wrenched off and I went into a tight spin. Below 10,000 feet I was thinking bailout before regaining control. This fiasco resulted in courts martial for the pilot who shot down Stein."

John Stein's story does not end here. In fact, the files were not closed on this tragedy until the Spring of 1949, when he was finally interred at the US Military Cemetery at Neuville en Condroz in Neuville, Belgium.

This is a marvelous example of how Graves Registration did its job in the Stein case. Their dedication and pure doggedness is an example of how it should have been accomplished in the Patton case.

Department of the Army files indicate that After Searby and Bope lost sight of John Stein's aircraft in the clouds, it continued on toward the earth and crashed. In their efforts to locate the crash sight, operating on information from Missing Aircrew Report MACR 437, US Army Graves Registration Investigators determined that John Stein's Mustang had crashed near the town of Gamborg, Denmark. Interviews with the locals indicated that the aircraft had landed in a body of water called Gamborg

Lake. It came to rest in an inlet about 250 wide, missing dry land by about 100 feet. The lake was only about 20 feet deep at this point.

According to a report from the Denmark Detachment of the Graves Registration Command dated 6 May 1948, the Danish Underground had attempted to recover the aircraft shortly after it had crashed. They attached cables to the fuselage and tried to pull it out with raw manpower but could only obtained small pieces. On the 6th of May 1948, another attempt was made to recover the aircraft using a hook and cable attached operated a winch on a heavy truck. A local Diver opined that diving operations necessary for the recovery was too dangerous because of the very deep mud in which the Mustang was buried. The US Army Investigator concluded that the aircraft and pilot were unrecoverable.

Graves Registration Commanders did not agree with the unrecoverable conclusions of the Investigator and in September 1948, a local contractor was hired to complete the recovery, It was a very difficult operation but it was successfully completed on 8 October 1948 and Lt. Stein was buried near the crash site. On 22 November 1948, he was reinterred at the US Military Cemetery at Nueville en Concroz, Belgium with the final identification made on 20 June 1949. Final interment at Nueville USMC took place on 15 November 1949.

Another interesting element of this story comes in the form of the loss of 1st Scouting Force pilot, William E. Cox (MACR 8420) on the same day, 3 April 1945, in the same area as Lt. Stein went down. The connection between the 2 lost airmen comes in a Graves registration document dated 11 June 1948 which speculated that the aircraft found in Gamborg Lake might be that of Lt. Cox. This position was held be the investigators until the remains were identified as Lt. Stein.

James Reed is Missing In Action

On 9 April, still smarting from the loss of John Stein, the Scouts were dealt another blow when James H. Reed, who had joined the unit only a few days before, was lost in the English Channel after he bailed out from his crippled Mustang.

The mission was number 130 for the 3rd Scouting Force and the target was Munich, Neuberg. The mission log reads as follows:

Lt. Reed, no. 2 man in Kodak White Flight, lead by Lt. Searby, experienced some trouble on return in attempting to drop his wing tanks and although White Leader told him to bail out while he still had 4000 feet, Lt. Reed evidently misunderstood or did not hear and rode his ship into the channel. The results of a prolonged search of the area were nil. Lt. Reed was never recovered and is MIA to this day.

Another Friendly Fire Incident

On 17 April, another friendly fire incident occurred with a near-victim being a member of the 8th Air Force Command Staff. Jack Hitt provided this description of the incident which occurred on a mission to Dresden. It was typical Scouting Force effort which required the 3rd Scouting Force Flight to lead the bombers to Dresden-Neustadt/Aussig/Roundice targets. The non-standard aspect of this mission was that Major General Earl Partridge 3rd Air Division Commander was to accompany the flight. General Partridge was a big booster of the Scouting Force concept and wanted to get the feel of a typical scouting mission. The Scouting Force, consisting of Jack Hitt, Kenneth Bope, Joe Nelson, Dick Jacobson, Ted Williams, Cliff Manlove, Ed Unger and Davis Difley, were a bit nervous with the "big man" on board but all went well, for the first half of the mission. The Scouts, did their usual fine job, logging over 2 hours actual instrument time in leading the bombers thru the weather. Over 400 bombers from the 3rd Air division went to the target, bombing effectively, while losing two of the B-17's and having damage to 47 others.

On the return trip, nearing the Channel coast all was going well and the Scouts were allowing themselves the luxury of a sigh of relief, when a large group of American Mustangs appeared from the west. The Mustangs were preparing to attack when the fighter leader recognized the Scouts as Americans and pulled off; all except one eager beaver who pressed on, spraying .50 caliber rounds amongst the Scouting Force formation. Flight Leader, Ed Unger, chased the offender all the way back to his base in England to identify the culprit. No one in the Scouting Force was injured but General Partridge was understandingly chagrined. The fate of the offender is unrecorded but it is suspected that he had serious conversation with his Squadron and Group Commanders.

Tom Fitzsimmons is lost on the next-to-last day of combat operations- A 20 April mission sent the units emotions plummeting to its lowest level of the war when **Tom Fitzsimmons** was shot down by Allied gunners over Holland. This was especially tragic since Tom was on his final mission of his 2nd tour with the Scouts and the next-to-last mission flown by the 3rd Scouting Force. The Flight was returning from a mission to Oranienburg and had just passed over the Dutch border. They were flying at 25,000 foot altitude when Tom announced that he was going down to the deck to take a look at the war in Holland. This was a fatal error for as soon as he approached the outskirts of Maargraten, at a low altitude, the Antiaircraft guns opened up and his Mustang was hit in the tail, which immediately separated from the aircraft and the fatal crash was instantaneous.

Tom's death was an especially hard blow for LuVerne Abendroth, Tom's best friend. They had been together since flight training and had come overseas together in 1943 with Laverne as Pilot and Tom as Co-Pilot of a B-24. Although they were eventually assigned to different Bomb Groups. LuVerne to the 493rd and Tom to the 486th, they had always maintained a close communication and were together as much as the war allowed. Luverne was one of the original Scouts, entering the unit in August 1944 and was quick to recruit him into the Scouting Force when Tom had completed his bomber tour.

Final Mission

The final mission for the 3rd Scouting Force was flown on 21 April 1945 in support of a fleets of 232 B-17's which bombed Landsberg, Amlech and Ingolstadt Germany.

The complete history of the Scouts may be found in the publication: FIGHTING SCOUTS OF THE 8TH AIR FORCE 1944-1945 BY E. RICHARD ATKINS and Volume 2 which is expected to be available in late 2007.

Printed in the United States
By Bookmasters